AWAKENED AND UNLEASHED

A JOURNEY OF SELF-DISCOVERY

SHELLISE BERRY

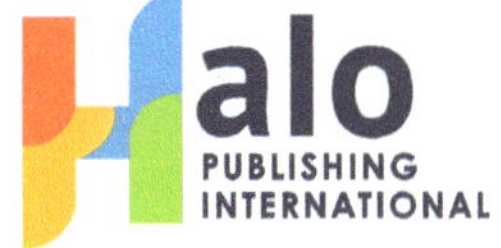

Halo
PUBLISHING
INTERNATIONAL

ISBN: 978-1-61244-936-4
LCCN: 2020921264

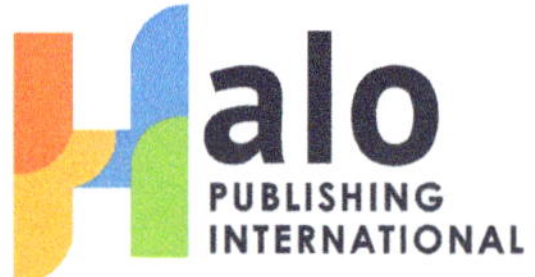

Halo Publishing International, LLC
8000 W Interstate 10, Suite 600
San Antonio, Texas 78230
www.halopublishing.com

Printed and bound in the United States

I am thankful to God for providing
the inspiration and my ability to paint.

I would like to thank my husband, Andre, and my sons,
Chris and Micchi, for all of their support.

Thank you to my mother, Dora McKinney,
for helping me when I got writer's block.

I would like to thank my photographer, Joyce Shelton
of Jems Photography. http://www.jemsphoto.com/

I would like to thank my editor, Jessica Gutierrez,
for all of her hard work.

Contents

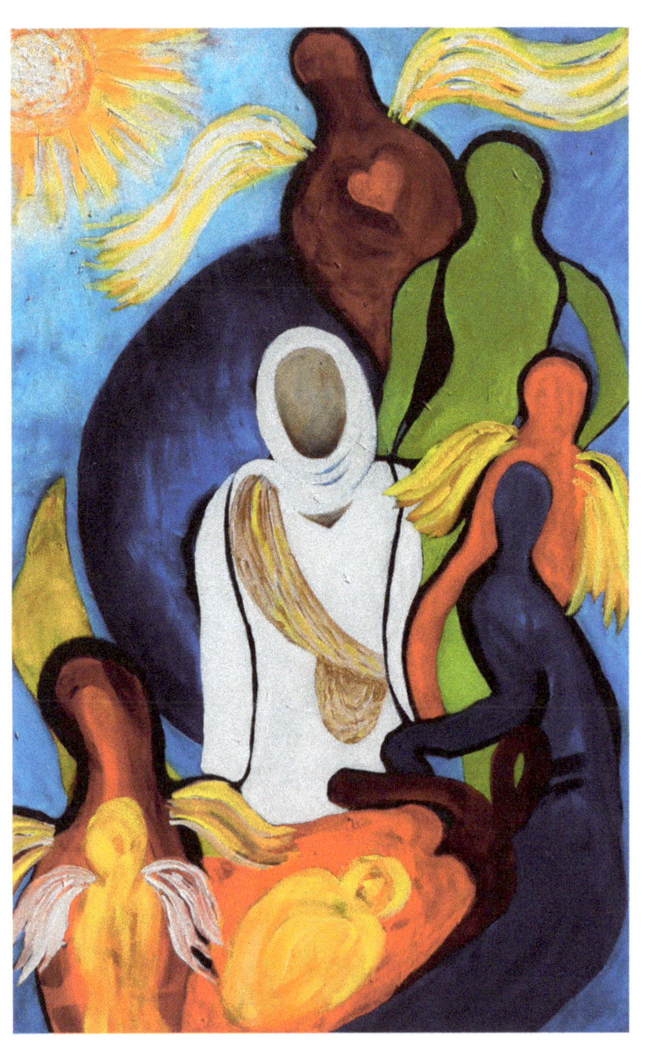

"It is Done"

Luke 24:27 (AMP) "Then beginning with Moses and [throughout] all the [writings of the] prophets, He explained *and* interpreted for them the things referring to Himself [found] in all the Scriptures."

Revelation 21:6 (AMP) "And He said to me, 'It is done. I am the Alpha and the Omega, the Beginning and the End. To the one who thirsts I will give [water] from the fountain of the water of life without cost.'"

You may have been taught that there is no guarantee you will make it into heaven. You may believe that you have to complete an indeterminate number of good deeds to qualify for an eternity with God. Or it may be your opinion that your good deeds only need to outweigh your bad ones for you to get entry through the pearly gates. All of these beliefs are false. The Bible declares that Jesus paid the price for your salvation through the shedding of His blood. His virgin birth and ultimate sacrifice were foretold hundreds of years before He was born. It is His blood that secures a place for you with God for eternity.

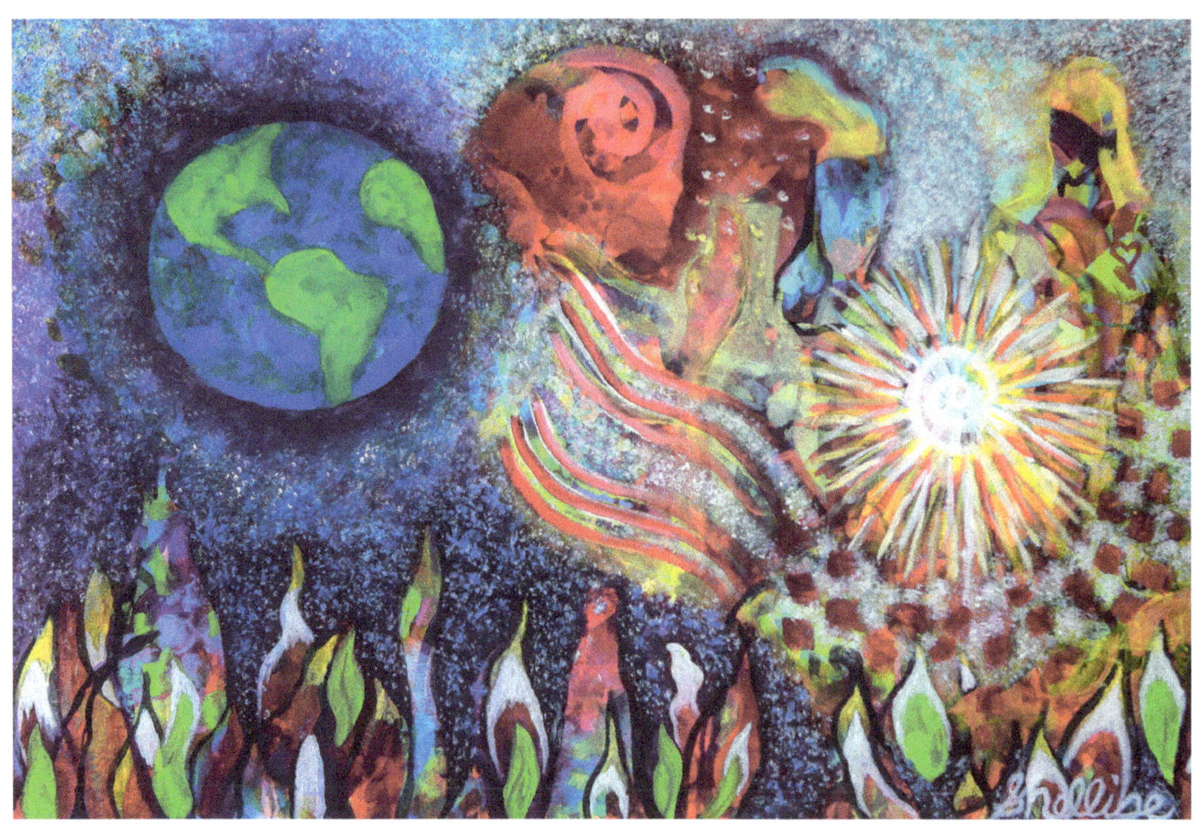

"Choose"

Joshua 24:15 (AMP) "'If it is unacceptable in your sight to serve the Lord, choose for yourselves this day whom you will serve: whether the gods which your fathers served that were on the other side of the River, or the gods of the Amorites in whose land you live; but as for me and my house, we will serve the Lord.'"

Everyone serves someone or something either by choice or involuntarily. Some individuals serve and idolize movie stars, musicians, or athletes, while others focus on material things, such as cars, houses, jewelry, and money. None of these people or things will bring you satisfaction. As a child of God, your focus should be solely on Him. Any other focal point in your life will lead to enslavement to that item and discontent. Loving God with all of your heart, soul, mind, and body is your duty as His child. Will you choose today as the day you make God the center of your attention and life?

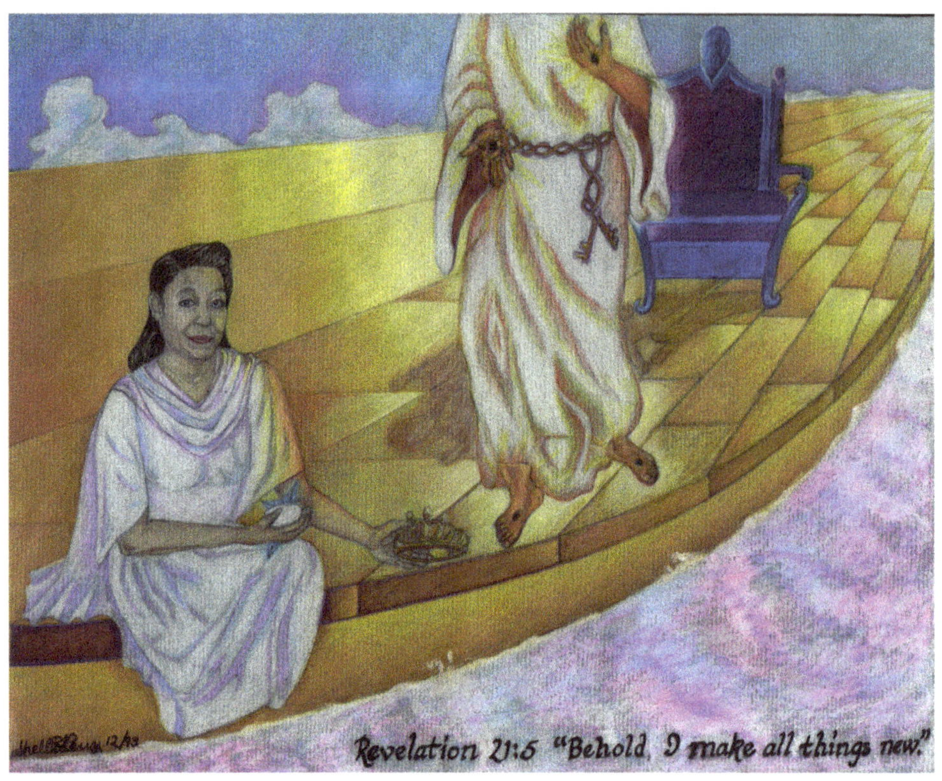

"Heaven"

Revelation 21:5 (AMP) "And He who sits on the throne said, 'Behold, I am making all things new.'"

Heaven isn't a make-believe place. It is a place God created. Jesus went there to prepare a place where you can spend eternity. In heaven, all things will be made new. No more sickness, pain, or death. It will be a place of joy and happiness, with no tears or sorrow. With a simple choice in life, you can receive the promise to be made new for eternity. Just follow the ABCs of Salvation:

<u>A is for Admit.</u> Admit that you have done wrong. In other words, you have sinned. A sin is any thought or action that disobeys God.

<u>B is for Believe.</u> You must believe in your heart that Jesus came, died, and rose again to pay the price for your sins.

<u>C is for Choose and Confess.</u> You must choose to trust Jesus to be your Savior and guide your life. Finally, confess with your mouth that He is Lord! By taking these three steps, you are now a child of God! Welcome to the family!

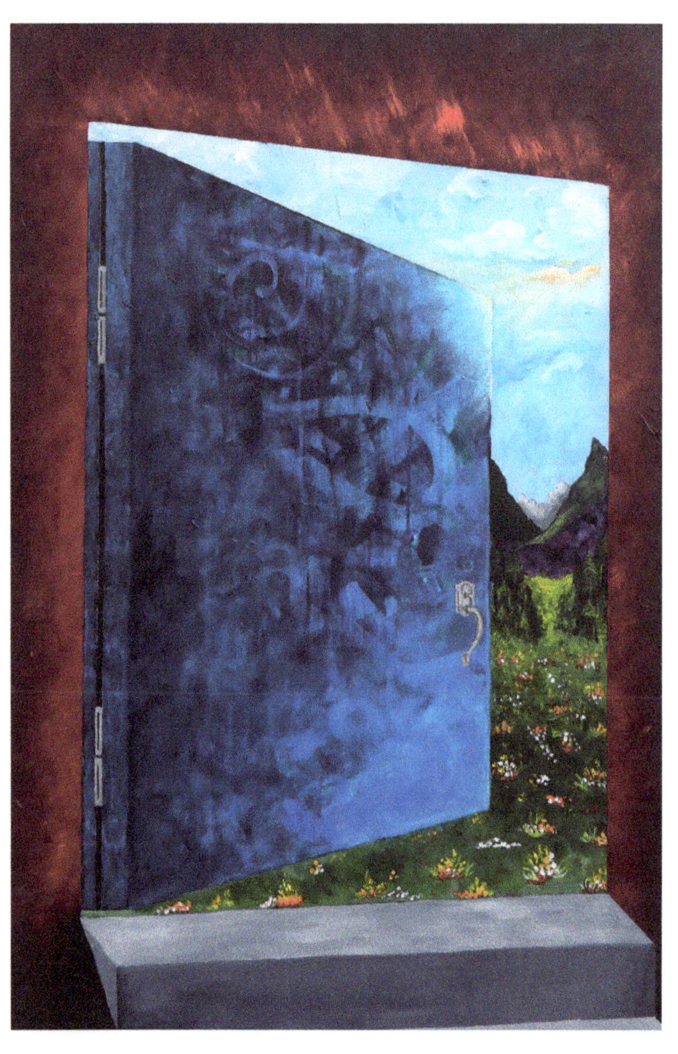

"Knock"

Revelation 3:20 (AMP) ""Behold, I stand at the door [of the church] and *continually* knock. If anyone hears My voice and opens the door, I will come in and eat with him (restore him), and he with Me.""

Have you been walking through life with your heart closed off to anything related to God? How have you been dealing with problems you have encountered? Do you feel spiritually empty? Is there a deep hunger inside of you that you don't know how to satisfy? Well, the answer to all of those questions is a relationship with Jesus Christ. Jesus came so you could have a full life. A life in which you don't have to walk alone. He is waiting patiently at the door of your heart. Jesus wants to help you live a full life here on Earth while He prepares a place for you in heaven. It is Jesus' desire to come into your heart and fill that void you have felt all your life. Listen! Do you hear the sound of Jesus quietly knocking on the door of your heart? He's waiting for you to invite Him in. Your life will never be the same.

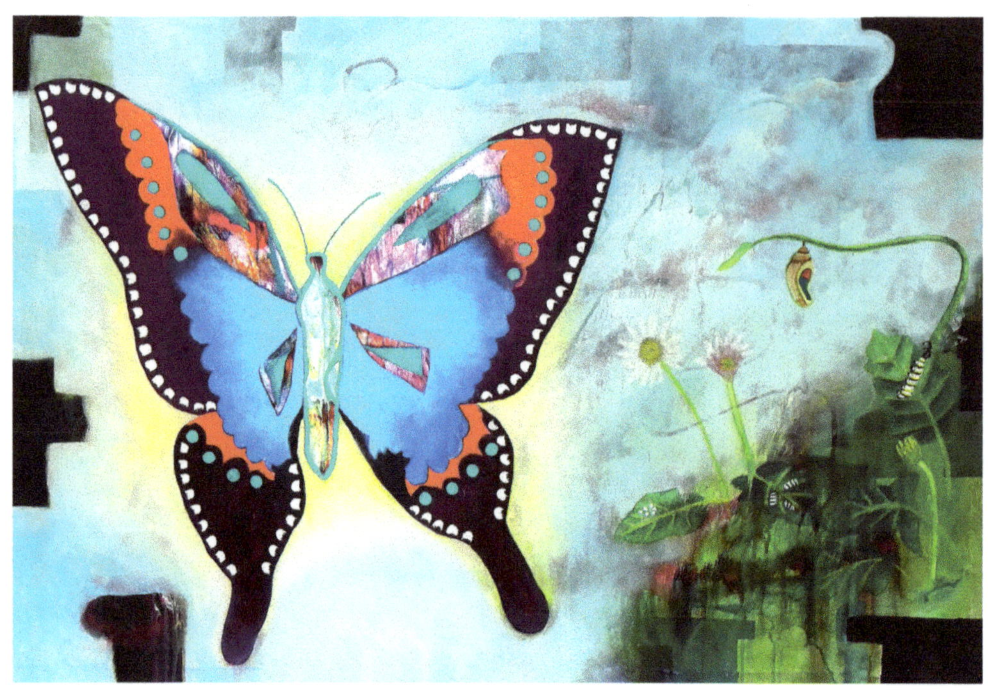

"Transformation"

Romans 12:2 (AMP) "And do not be conformed to this world [any longer with its superficial values and customs], but be transformed *and* progressively changed [as you mature spiritually] by the renewing of your mind [focusing on godly values and ethical attitudes], so that you may prove [for yourselves] what the will of God is, that which is good and acceptable and perfect [in His plan and purpose for you]."

Just as the butterfly goes through several steps before it can fly, we also must take steps to transform our lives.

1. Admit that your life needs to be changed. We have all made mistakes for which we need forgiveness.
2. You must believe that God exists and that His Son died for your sins and was raised again to life.
3. Confess with your mouth that Jesus Christ is Lord over your life.
4. Spend time praying and studying the Bible.
5. Spend time memorizing Scripture.

With just one touch from God, your mind will be renewed, and your life transformed.

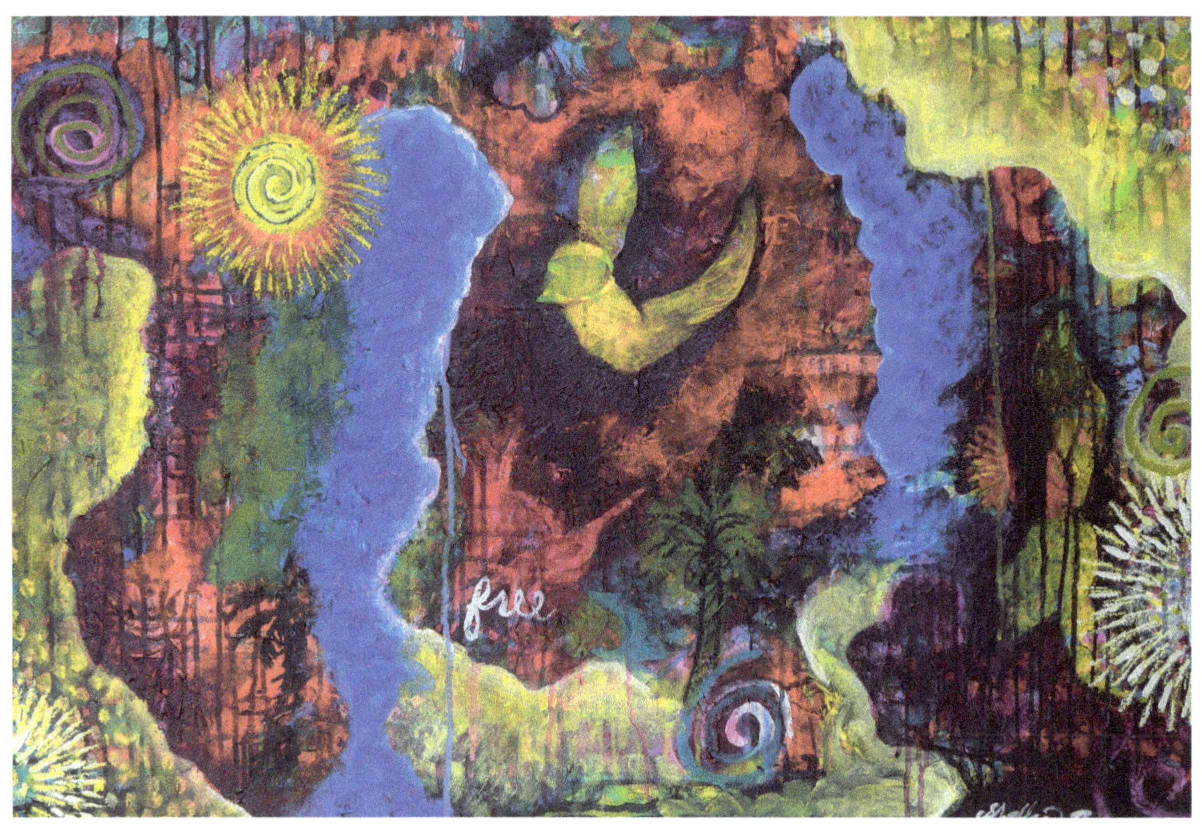

"Free"

John 8:36 (AMP) "'So if the Son makes you free, then you are unquestionably free.'"

Do you feel trapped by the problems of life? You may be dealing with emotional, physical, financial, or situational problems. These problems can cause physical and mental stress on your body and mind. Side effects may include anxiety, depression, cancer, high blood pressure, heart attacks, strokes, and even death.

You don't have to live in bondage, slave to the circumstances you face. Surrender your life to Jesus Christ, and He will help you through the stressors of life. You'll be free to start a new life.

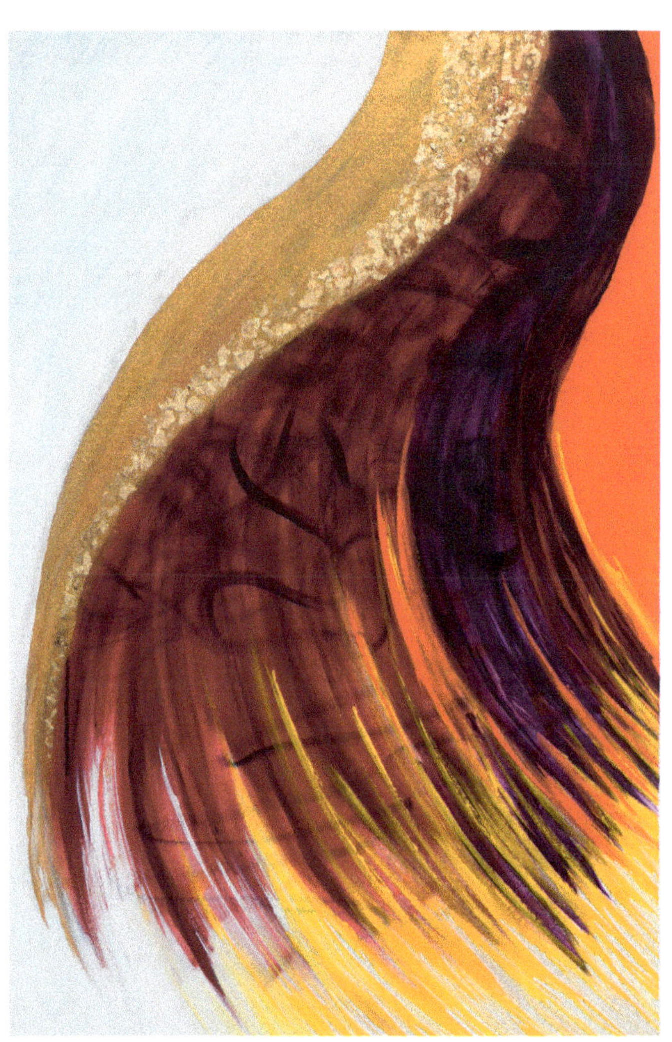

"In His Shadow"

Psalms 36:7 (KJV) "How excellent is thy lovingkindness, O God! therefore the children of men put their trust under the shadow of thy wings."

One of the main emphases of the Bible is God's lovingkindness toward humanity, His greatest creation. The Bible is the guideline for becoming more like Jesus every day, in preparation for eternity. God's Word, the Bible, provides assurance of His love, compassion, and trustworthiness. Because you are under the shadow of His wings, you are able to trust Him with all aspects of your life. Have you decided to follow Jesus?

"A New Creature"

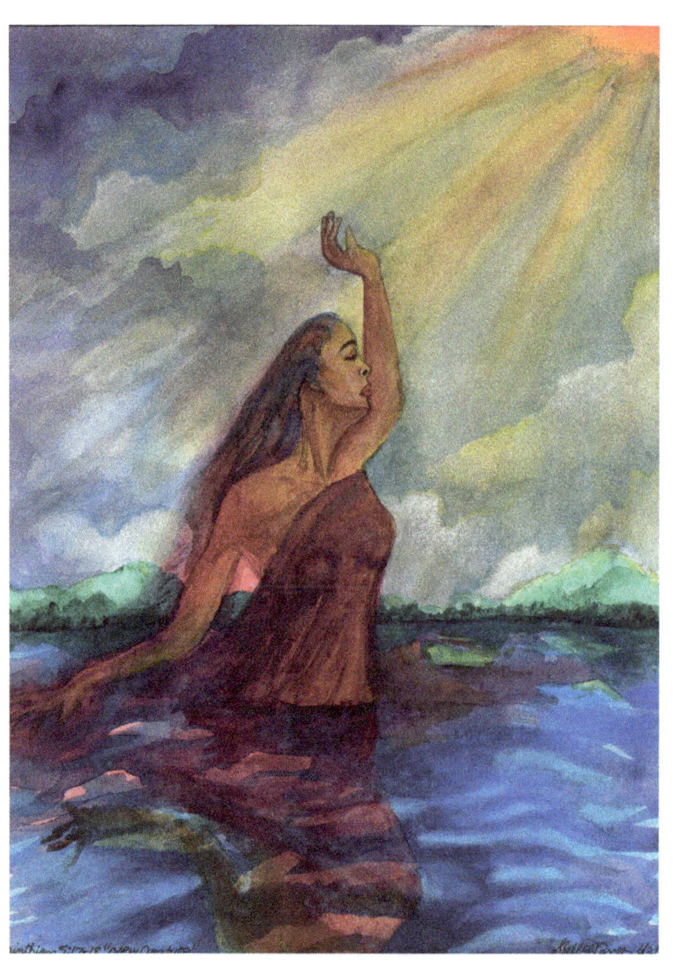

2 Corinthians 5:17 (AMP) "Therefore if anyone is in Christ [that is, grafted in, joined to Him by faith in Him as Savior], *he is* **a new creature [reborn and renewed by the Holy Spirit]; the old things [the previous moral and spiritual condition] have passed away. Behold, new things have come [because spiritual awakening brings a new life]."**

Regardless of your past mistakes, you have a chance for a new life if you make a simple choice. Choose to let Jesus Christ live in your heart and guide your life. Everything you have done wrong in your life will be erased. What is holding you back from starting a new life with Christ? Sometimes you may feel more comfortable with the situation in which you are currently living than you are with the unknown (a new life with Christ). Don't stay stuck in your past. Accept Christ as your Savior today and begin your new life.

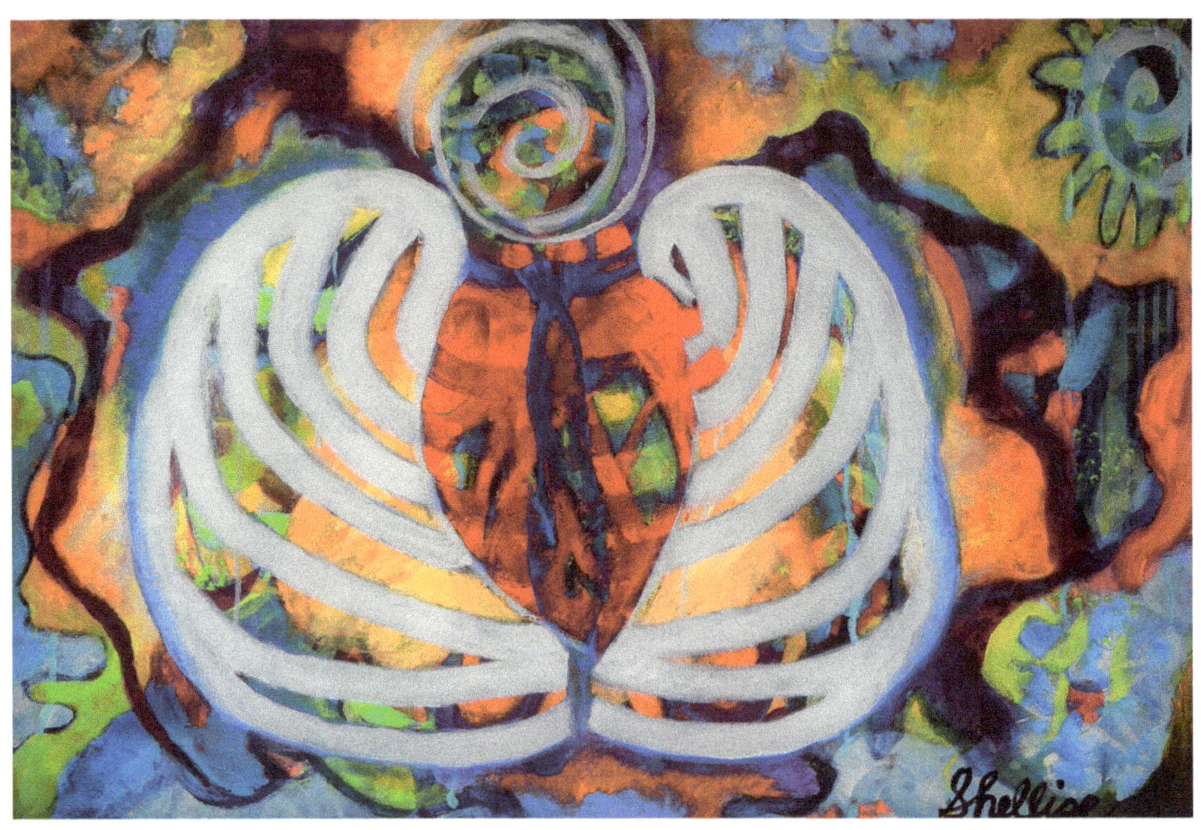

"New Heart"

Ezekiel 36:26 (MSG) **""""I'll give you a new heart, put a new spirit in you. I'll remove the stone heart from your body and replace it with a heart that's God-willed, not self-willed.""""**

Do you have a heart condition? Are you following God's will, or are you living life your way? The Word of God says that those living life their way have a stone for a heart. It is impossible to live a God-willed life without major surgery on your heart. All you have to do to correct your condition is surrender your heart to God and accept Jesus. God will then give you a new heart. A heart that is able to serve Him. Are you ready for your procedure?

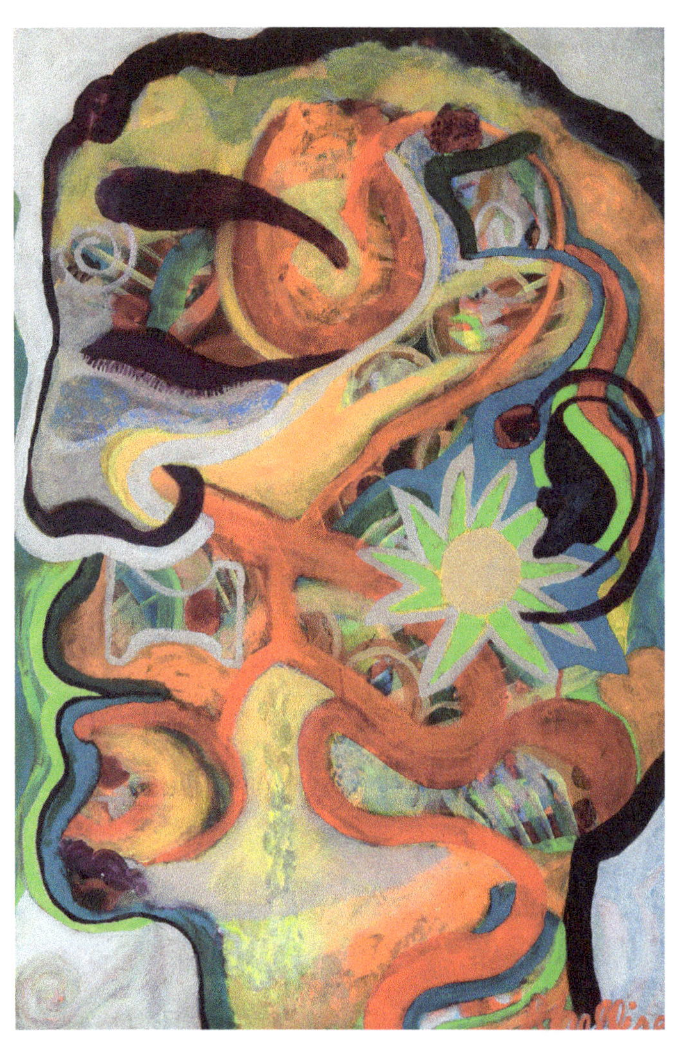

"First Breath"

Genesis 2:7 (AMP) "…then the LORD God formed [that is, created the body of] man from the dust of the ground, and breathed into his nostrils the breath of life; and the man became a living being [an individual complete in body and spirit]."

God created you in His image. You are a spirit being, a soul that resides in a physical body. Just as Adam became a living being when God breathed the first breath into his nostrils, you became spiritually alive when you accepted Jesus as your Lord and Savior. As a living being, you were created to live your life with complete dependency on God, your Father. You are to trust Him to supply your every need, including your next breath.

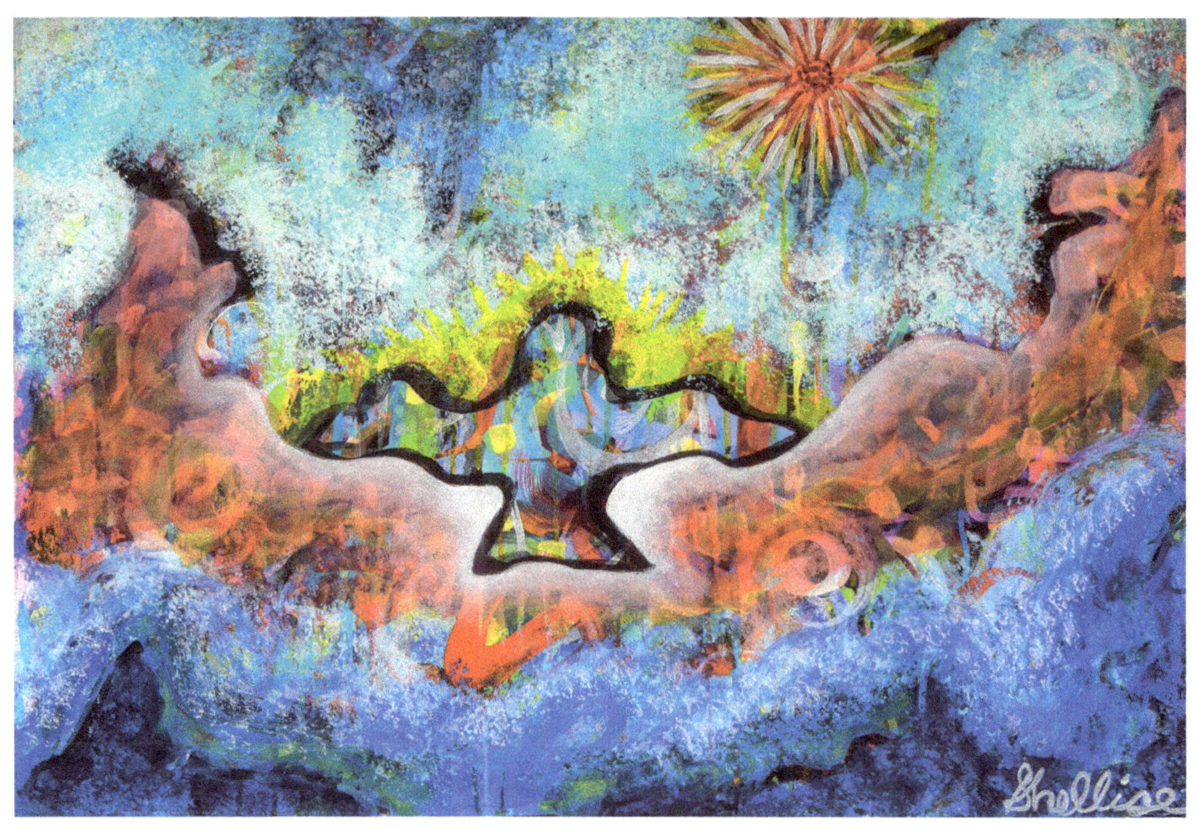

"Dove"

Luke 3:22 (AMP) "…and the Holy Spirit descended on Him in bodily form like a dove, and a voice came from heaven, 'You are My Son, My Beloved, in You I am well-pleased *and* delighted!'"

If you have accepted Jesus Christ into your life as your Lord and Savior, you have been adopted into the family of God. You are now a daughter of the Almighty God, and as His child, God will send the Holy Spirit to dwell within you. It is the Holy Spirit's job to intercede on your behalf with God and to inspire and empower you to live a Christ-like life. This is so that one day, God, the Father, will say, "You are my daughter, my beloved. In you, I am well pleased and delighted!"

"Power"

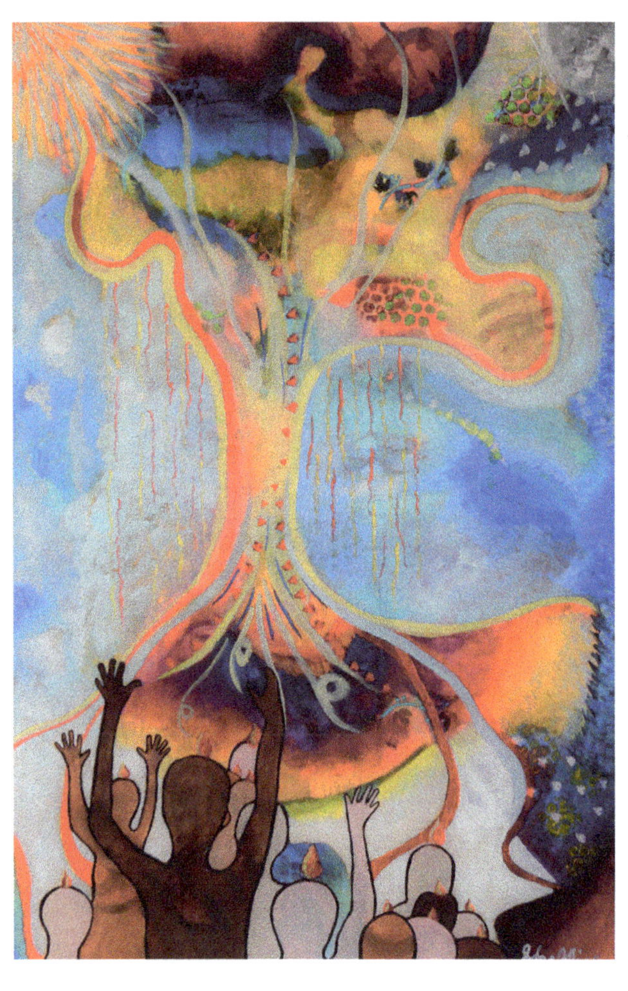

Acts 2:1-4 (AMP) "When the day of Pentecost had come, they were all together in one place, and suddenly a sound came from heaven like a rushing violent wind, and it filled the whole house where they were sitting. There appeared to them tongues resembling fire, which were being distributed [among them], and they rested on each one of them [as each person received the Holy Spirit]. And they were all filled [that is, diffused throughout their being] with the Holy Spirit and began to speak in other tongues (different languages), as the Spirit was giving them the ability to speak out [clearly and appropriately]."

As a daughter of the King, you are entitled to receive all of the gifts associated with that position. The Father offers you the power of the Holy Ghost. This power enables you to live a Christ-like life and will give you the ability to become a witness for Jesus throughout the world. After you have accepted Jesus as your Savior, you only need to invite the Holy Ghost to come and fill your heart. The Holy Ghost has many roles in the life of a believer. He is to act as your comforter and will intercede for you with the Father. He will teach you the Word of God and help you understand and remember what you've learned. He brings any sin in your life to your attention so you can confess and turn away from it. He also gives spiritual gifts to believers, including wisdom, messages of knowledge, faith, healing, miracles, prophecies, discernment of spirits, the ability to speak other languages, and the ability to interpret other languages. Are you ready to live an empowered life? You only have to invite Him to fill you with His presence.

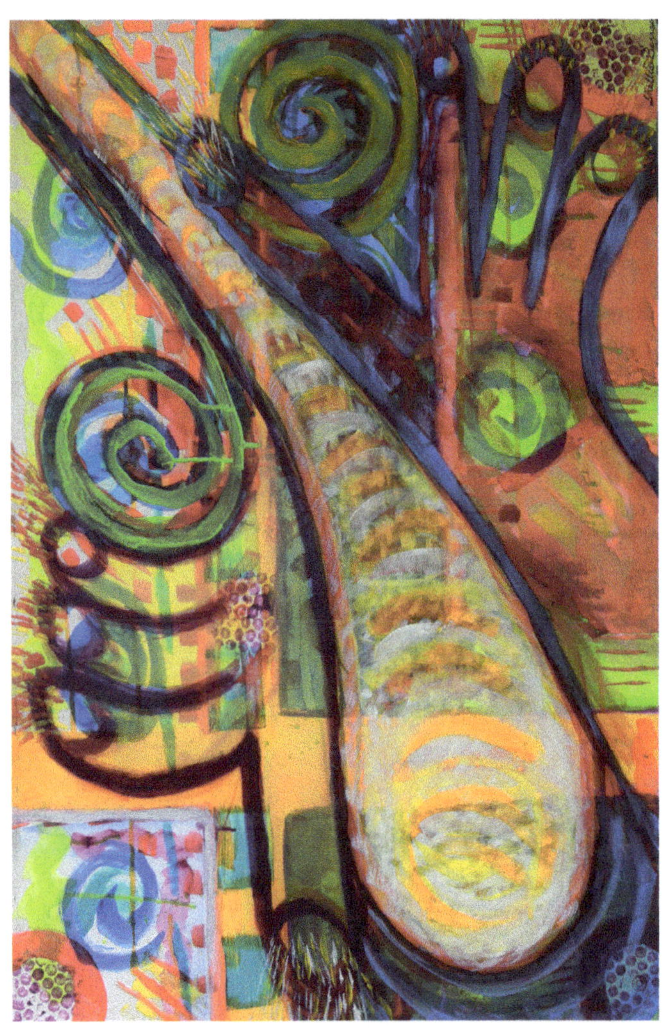

"Rained Down"

Acts 1:8 (AMP) "'But you will receive power *and* ability when the Holy Spirit comes upon you; and you will be My witnesses [to tell people about Me] both in Jerusalem and in all Judea, and Samaria, and even to the ends of the earth.'"

Before Jesus returned to heaven, He promised to send the Holy Spirit to live in the hearts of those who believe in Him. The Holy Spirit gives us the power to live a life that is pleasing to God. He gives us the ability to be transformed so that we begin to look like Jesus. The Holy Spirit also gives us gifts and talents that we need to use to spread the good news of Jesus' sacrifice of love. Are you living a life filled with and guided by the Holy Spirit? You only need to ask Jesus to come into your heart, and then you will receive the gift of the indwelling of the Holy Spirit.

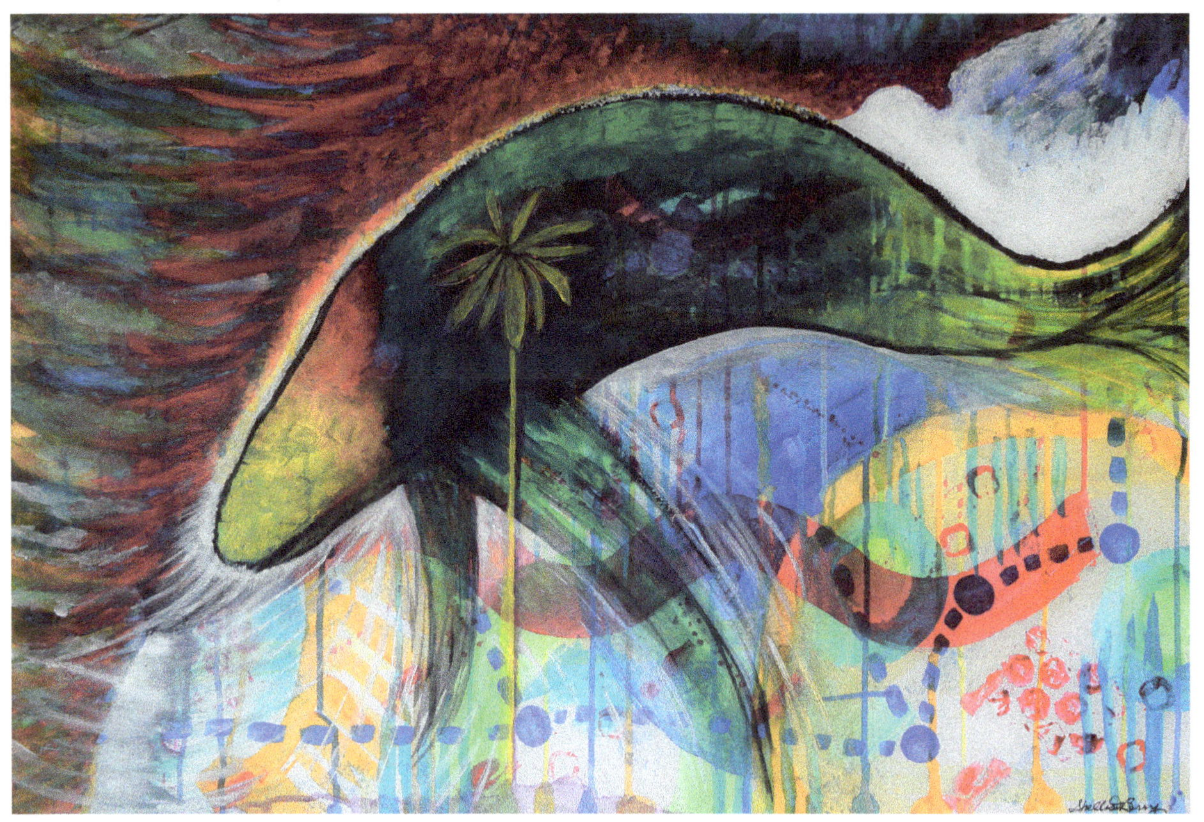

" 5ᵗʰ Day "

Genesis 1:21-23 (KJV) "And God created great whales, and every living creature that moveth, which the waters brought forth abundantly, after their kind, and every winged fowl after his kind: and God saw that it was good. And God blessed them, saying, Be fruitful, and multiply, and fill the waters in the seas, and let fowl multiply in the earth. And the evening and the morning were the fifth day."

Just as the whales were created for the sea and the birds for the skies, you were uniquely created by God. You were born at a certain place and time and are meant to fulfill a specific purpose. You were created for good. God designed you and gave you special gifts and talents to be used to benefit mankind and to bring glory to His Kingdom. Once Christ has become a part of your life, God sends the Holy Spirit to help you each and every day. He will help you make the right choices as you proceed toward achieving your purpose.

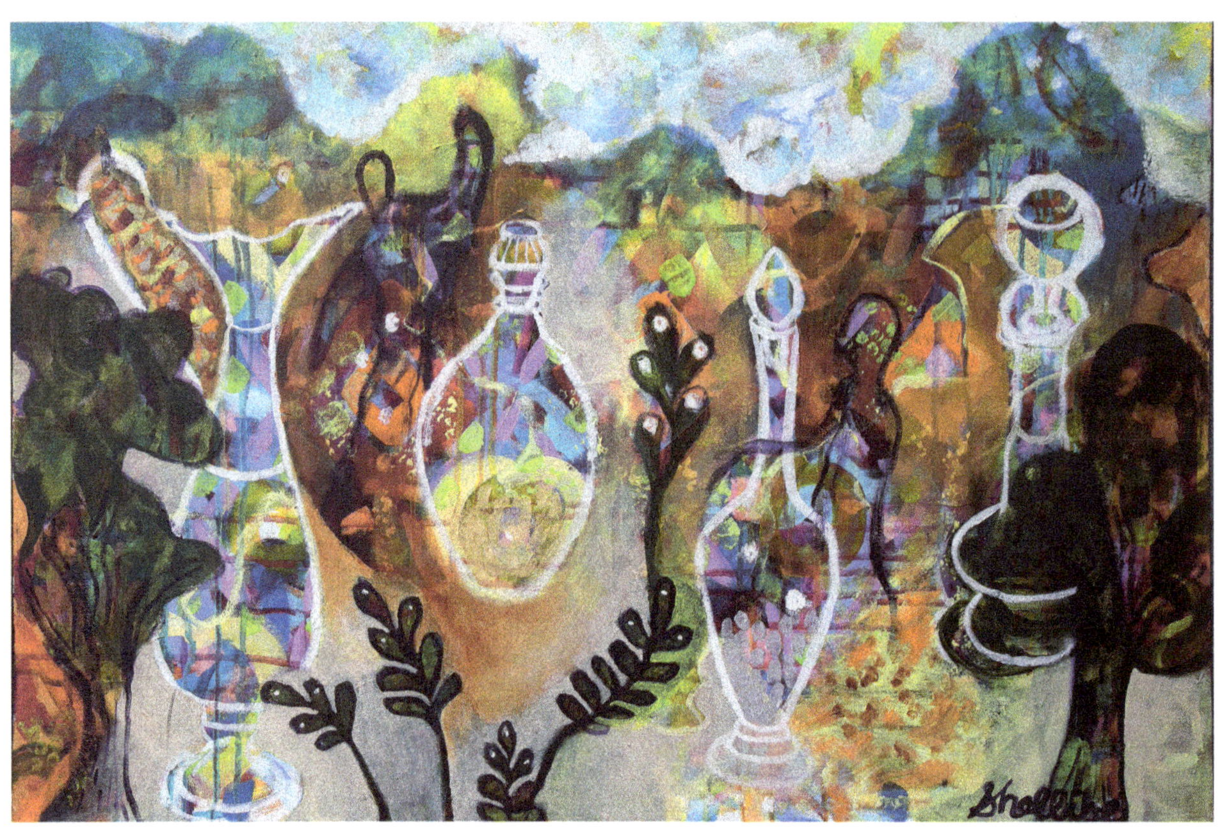

"Vessels"

2 Timothy 2:20-21 (AMP) "Now in a large house there are not only vessels *and* objects of gold and silver, but also vessels *and* objects of wood and of earthenware, and some are for honorable (noble, good) use and some for dishonorable (ignoble, common). Therefore, if anyone cleanses himself from these *things* [which are dishonorable— disobedient, sinful], he will be a vessel for honor, sanctified [set apart for a special purpose and], useful to the Master, prepared for every good work."

God created you to be uniquely different from any other person. You are a special vessel that was designed to complete a specific assignment while here on Earth. Has God already revealed to you the assignment you are meant to complete for His Kingdom? You may have a strong desire deep inside your heart to complete a specific task for God. Have you answered His call for service? What's holding you back? What are you waiting for? He chose you because you are perfect for the assignment! Three, two, one, GO!

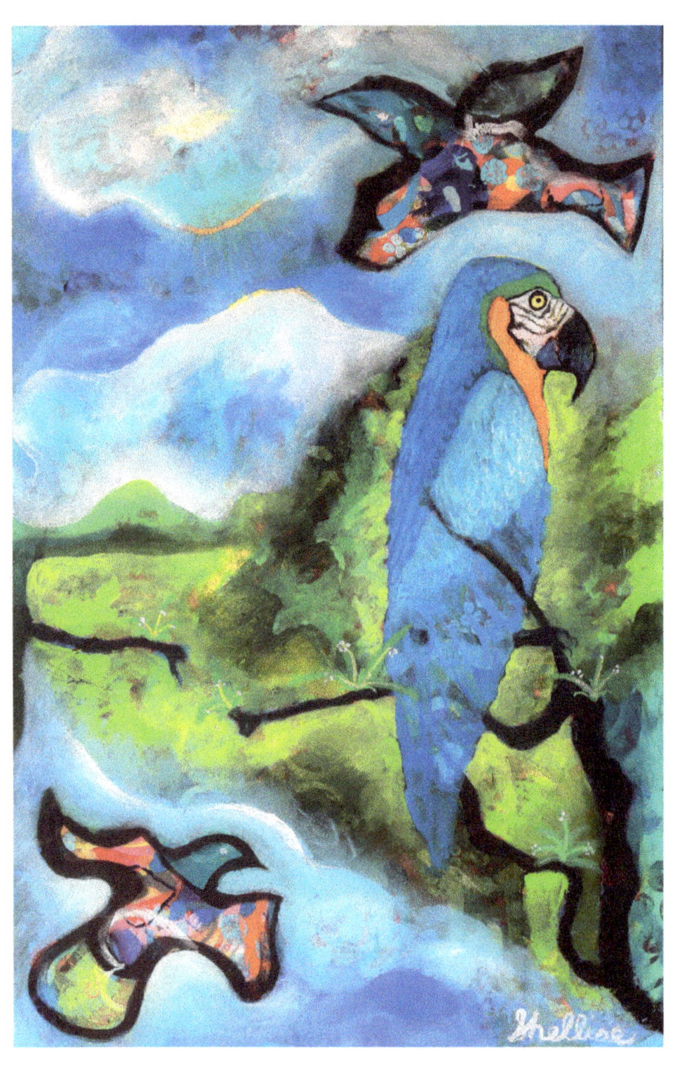

"5ᵗʰ Day #2"

Genesis 1:21-23 (AMP) "God created the great sea monsters and every living creature that moves, with which the waters swarmed according to their kind, and every winged bird according to its kind; and God saw that it was good *and* He affirmed and sustained it. And God blessed them, saying, 'Be fruitful, multiply, and fill the waters in the seas, and let birds multiply on the earth.' And there was evening and there was morning, a fifth day."

According to bird watchers and scientists, there are between nine and ten thousand species of birds in the world.[1] This entire collection of birds was created by God on the fifth day. He designed each one to be uniquely different. They didn't evolve over time into this vast abundance of birds. Our amazing Creator is all powerful. Look at the measures He took to create so many species of birds. Just imagine, from the beginning of time, there has only been one you! You are His greatest masterpiece!

---

[1] "New Study Doubles the Estimate of Bird Species in the World," American Museum of Natural History, accessed October 27, 2020, https://www.amnh.org/about/press-center/new-study-doubles-the-estimate-of-bird-species-in-the-world/.

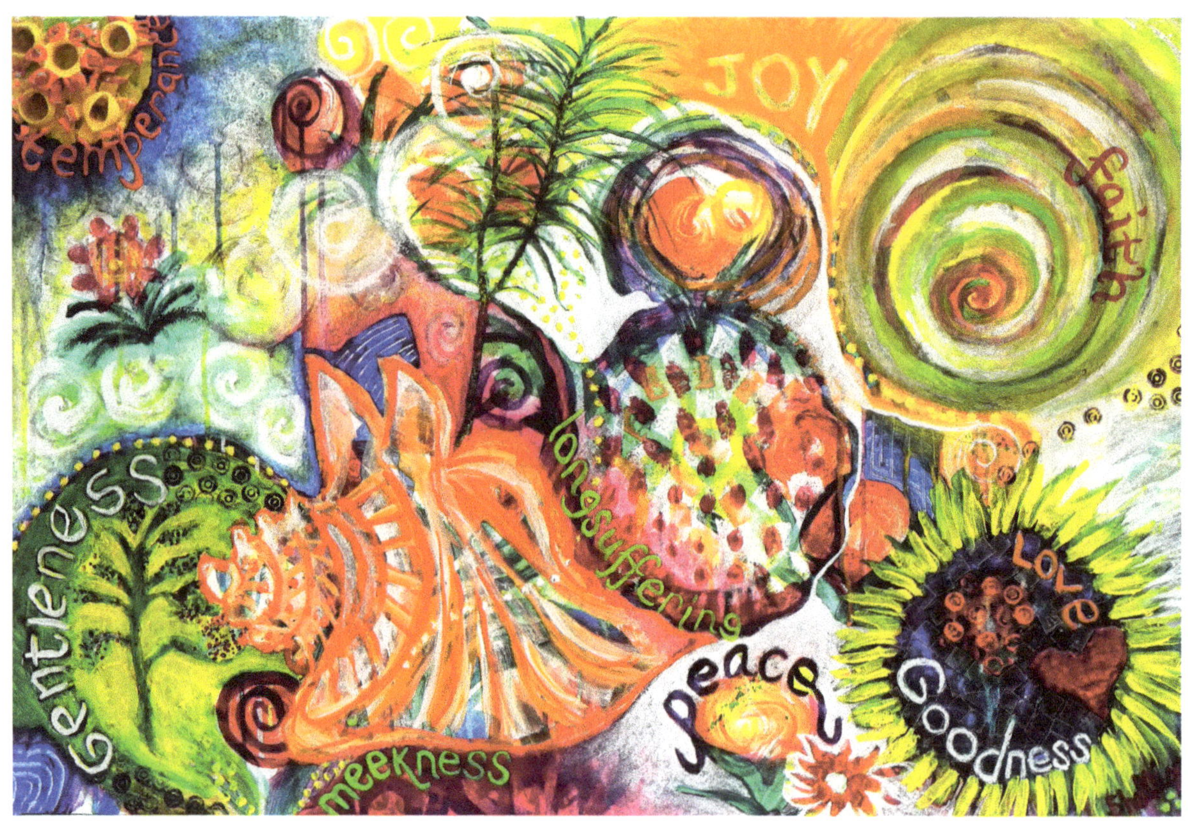

"Fruit"

Galatians 5:22-23 (AMP) "But the fruit of the Spirit [the result of His presence within us] is love [unselfish concern for others], joy [inner], peace, patience [not the ability to wait, but how we act while waiting], kindness, goodness, faithfulness, gentleness, self-control. Against such things there is no law."

As a result of your growing relationship with Jesus Christ, you will notice changes in your virtue and conduct. By continuing to let the Spirit of God direct your life, you will begin to develop new habits of the mind. These new habits include love, joy, peace, patience, kindness, goodness, faithfulness, gentleness, and self-control. These traits will become second nature. Developing these characteristics will produce a fulfilling life.

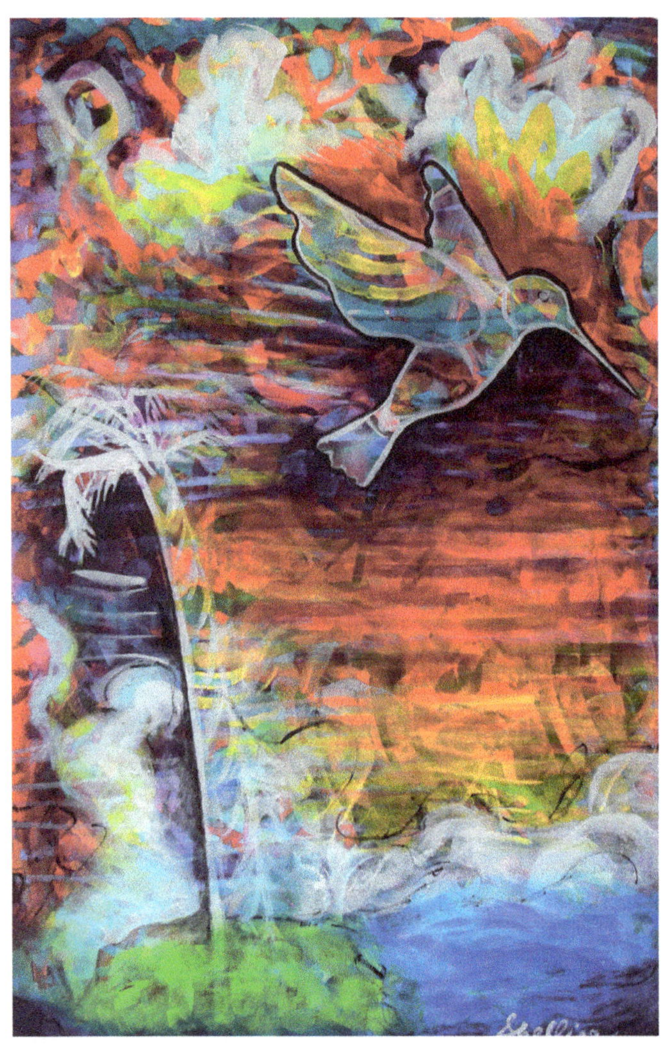

"Good News"

Mark 16:15 (AMP) "And He said to them, 'Go into all the world and preach the gospel to all creation.'"

Society is currently inundated with the constant flow of information coming from every direction. Often, the news broadcasted is unpleasant and discouraging. Before returning to heaven, Jesus commissioned His disciples to go around the world and proclaim the Gospel to every living creature. As an ambassador of Jesus Christ, you are required to declare the good news of Christ's love and ultimate sacrifice to everyone you encounter. Look at the hummingbird as an example. It flies to each flower, spreading life-giving pollen, in its search for nourishment. Imitate the amazing bird as you share the goodness of God's love and saving grace.

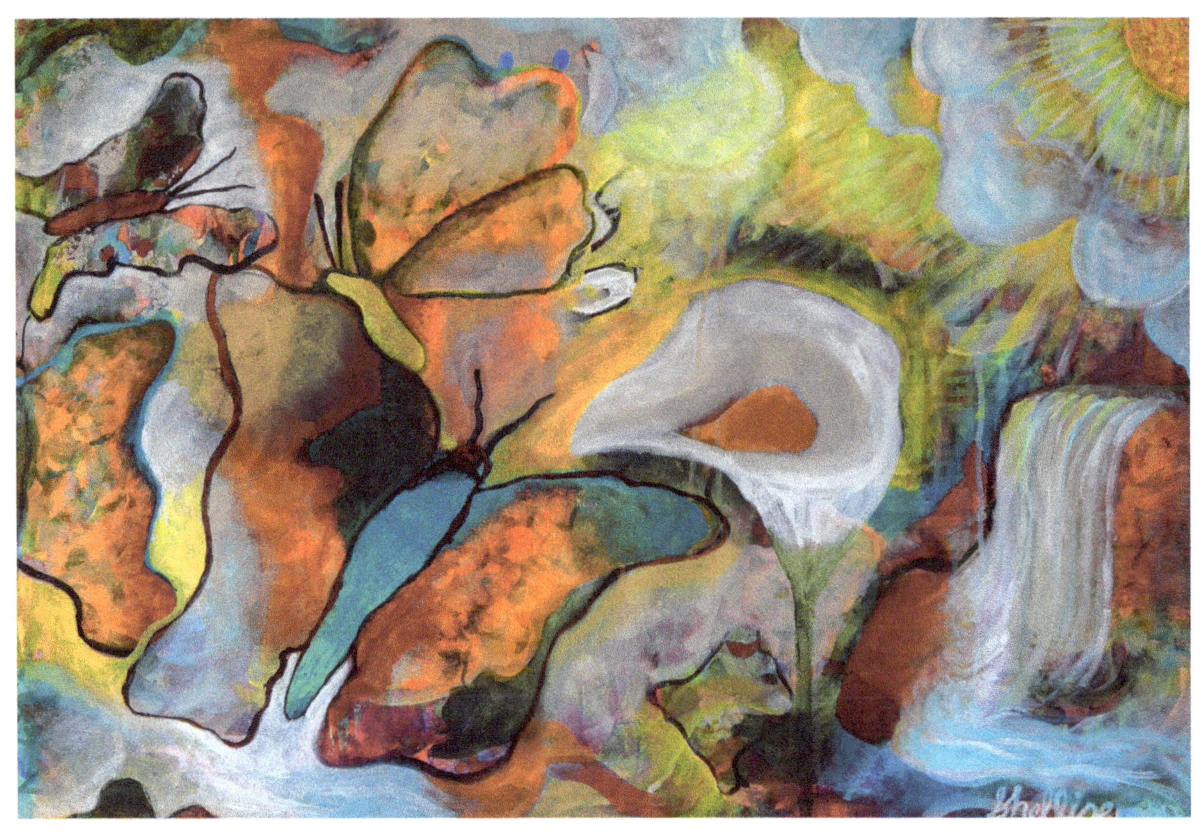

"Mercies"

Lamentations 3:22-23 (KJV) "It is of the Lord's mercies that we are not consumed, because his compassions fail not. They are new every morning: great is thy faithfulness."

Because our Creator loves us, He gives us an opportunity to start over with each new day. You don't have to be trapped in yesterday's problems or mistakes. Leave your issues from the day before in the past, where they belong. If God loves you enough to let you start over each day with new mercies, you should love Him enough to trust Him with your day-to-day living.

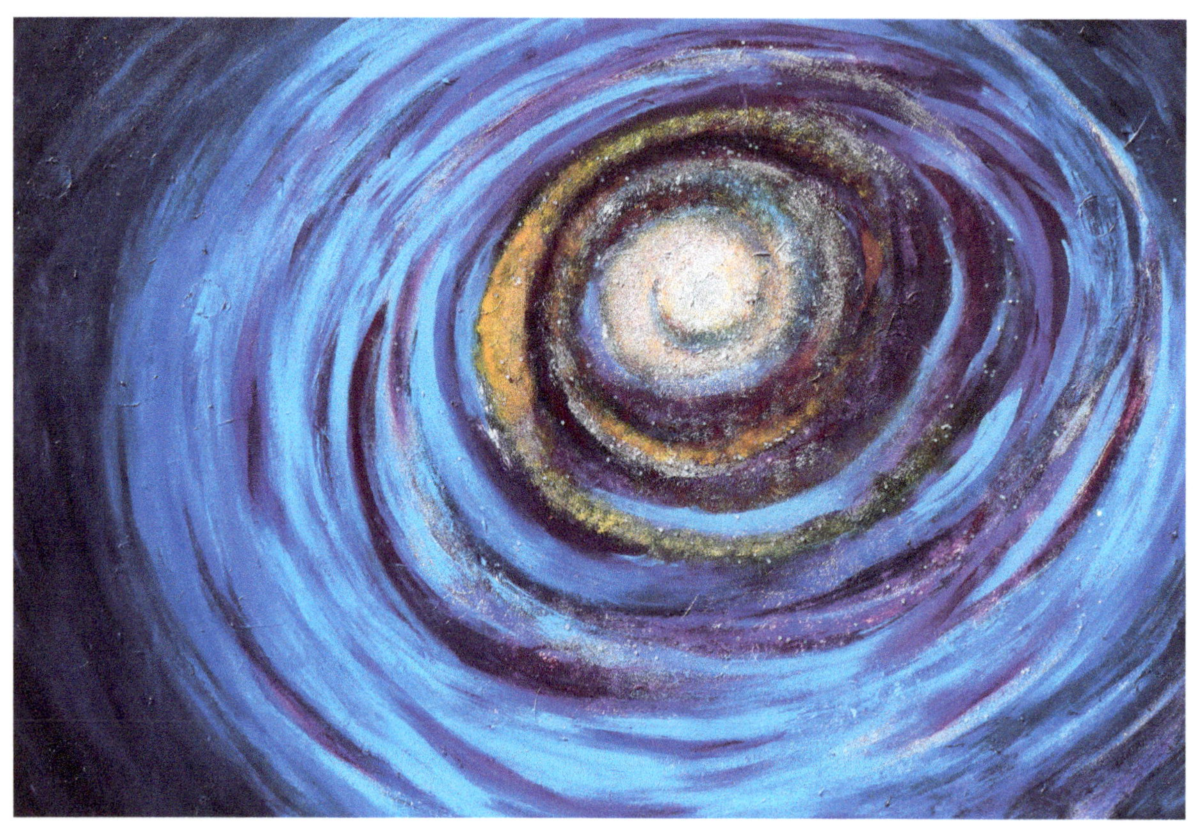

"Be Still"

Psalms 46:10 (AMP) "'Be still and know (recognize, understand) that I am God. I will be exalted among the nations! I will be exalted in the earth.'"

Is life making you feel anxious about tomorrow? You may be facing trials that seem to be coming from every direction. Stress on the job, a family crisis, car repairs, and financial hardships. When it rains, it pours. The bombardment of noises that are created in your mind by these troubles make it impossible to hear God. He is already working behind the scenes on your behalf. You only need to be still, breathe, and listen to what God is saying. God is in control.

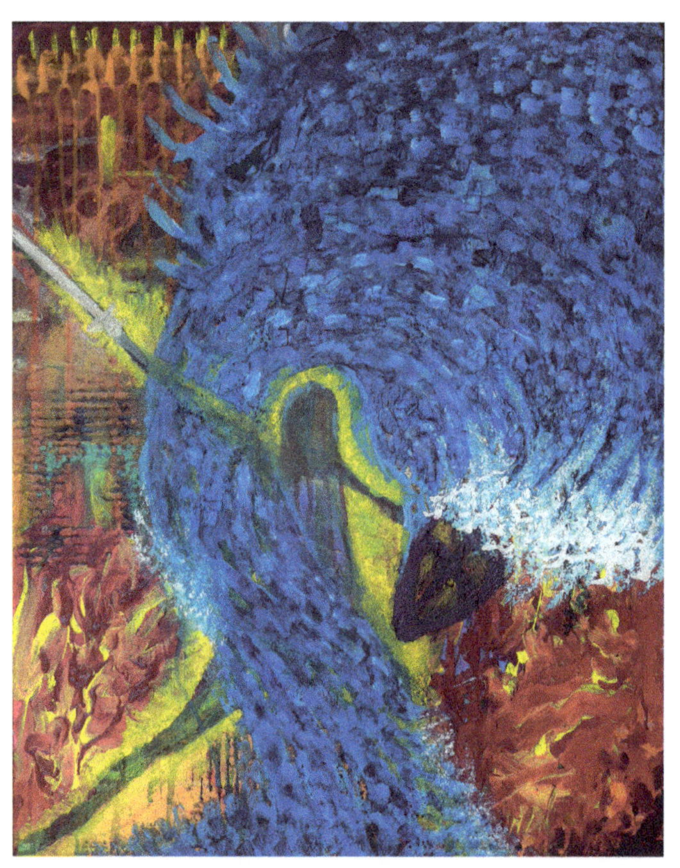

"Protection"

Isaiah 43:1-2 (AMP) "But now, this is what the LORD, your Creator says, O Jacob, And He who formed you, O Israel, 'Do not fear, for I have redeemed you [from captivity]; I have called you by name; you are Mine! When you pass through the waters, I will be with you; And through the rivers, they will not overwhelm you. When you walk through fire, you will not be scorched, Nor will the flame burn you.'"

God sent His Son, Jesus, to die for you as a payment for your sins. Because Jesus paid the ultimate price, you belong to Him. He promises to be with you and take care of you through all of the challenges of life. With God's protection, nothing will be too much for you to overcome. He promises you won't be buried under the weight of your problems.

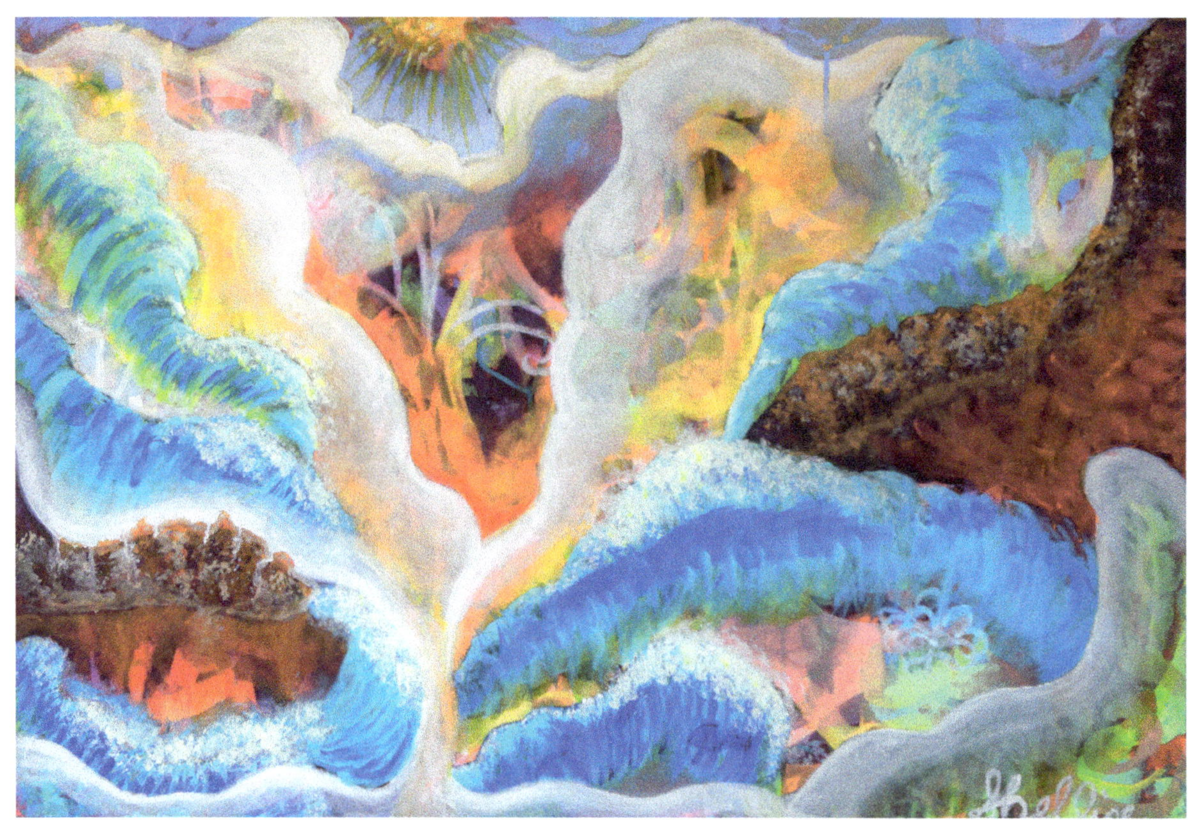

"Red Sea"

Exodus 14:21-22 (AMP) "Then Moses stretched out his hand over the sea; and the LORD swept the sea back by a strong east wind all that night and turned the seabed into dry land, and the waters were divided. The Israelites went into the middle of the sea on dry land, and the waters formed a wall to them on their right hand and on their left."

Often in life, you will be faced with obstacles that leave you feeling like you're stuck between two walls that are closing in on you. Your Father, the Creator, will protect you from the things that have you bound and enslaved. Don't stop to look around at the walls. Seek God with all of your heart. He will prepare a path to the other side of your troubles. You only need to keep your eyes on Him.

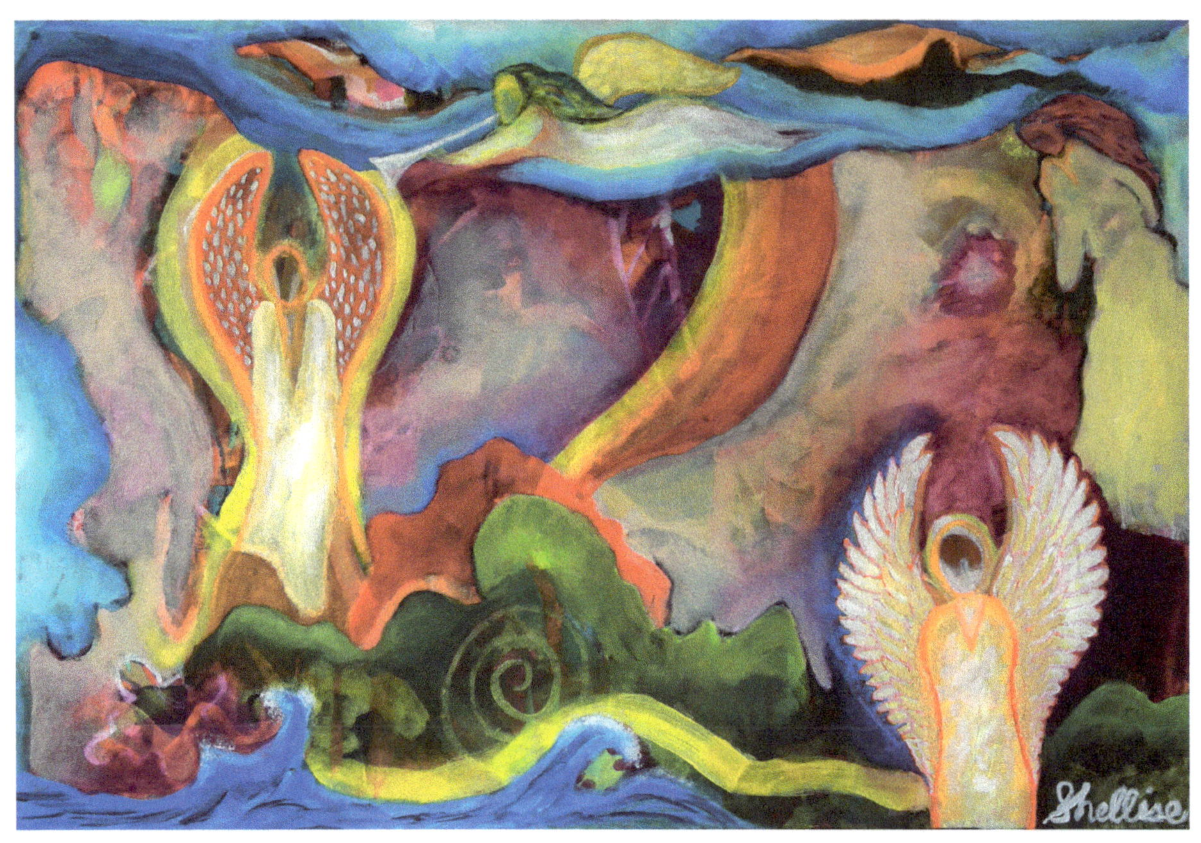

"Angels Watching"

Psalms 91:10-12 (MSG) "Evil can't get close to you, harm can't get through the door. He ordered his angels to guard you wherever you go. If you stumble, they'll catch you; their job is to keep you from falling."

Did you know that you are indestructible until your time on Earth is done? That's right! You're like Supergirl or Wonder Woman. Unstoppable! You might ask, how is that possible? It is because God has His angels assigned to you, keeping evil away and keeping you safe. Don't spend your time worrying about your well-being. Rest easy knowing that God sends His angels to watch over those He loves.

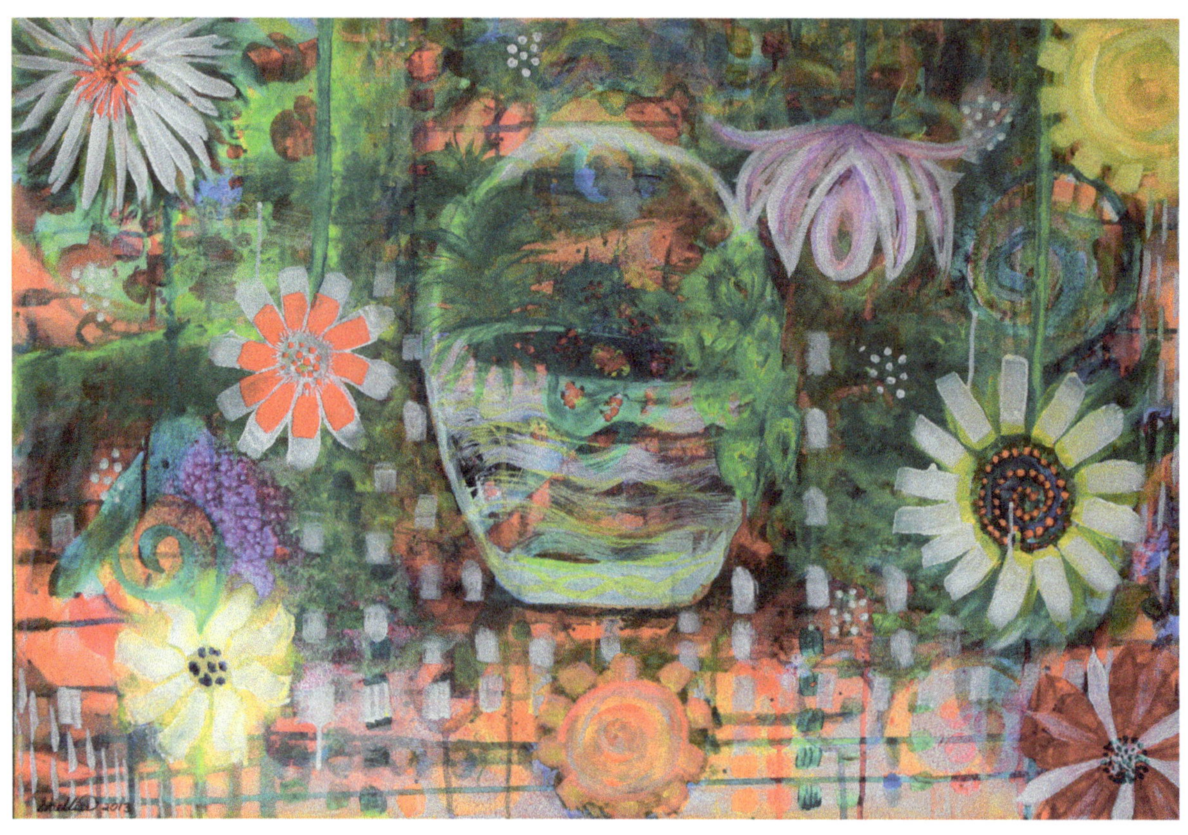

"Eden"

Genesis 2:8 (AMP) "And the Lᴏʀᴅ God planted a garden (oasis) in the east, in Eden (delight, land of happiness); and He put the man whom He had formed (created) there."

God created the Garden of Eden to meet every need of Adam and Eve. God's role as provider has not changed. He is the same God today as He was in the Garden. You are His child, and He loves you and wants to supply your every need. You only need to put your trust in His Son, Jesus. Will you trust in Jesus today?

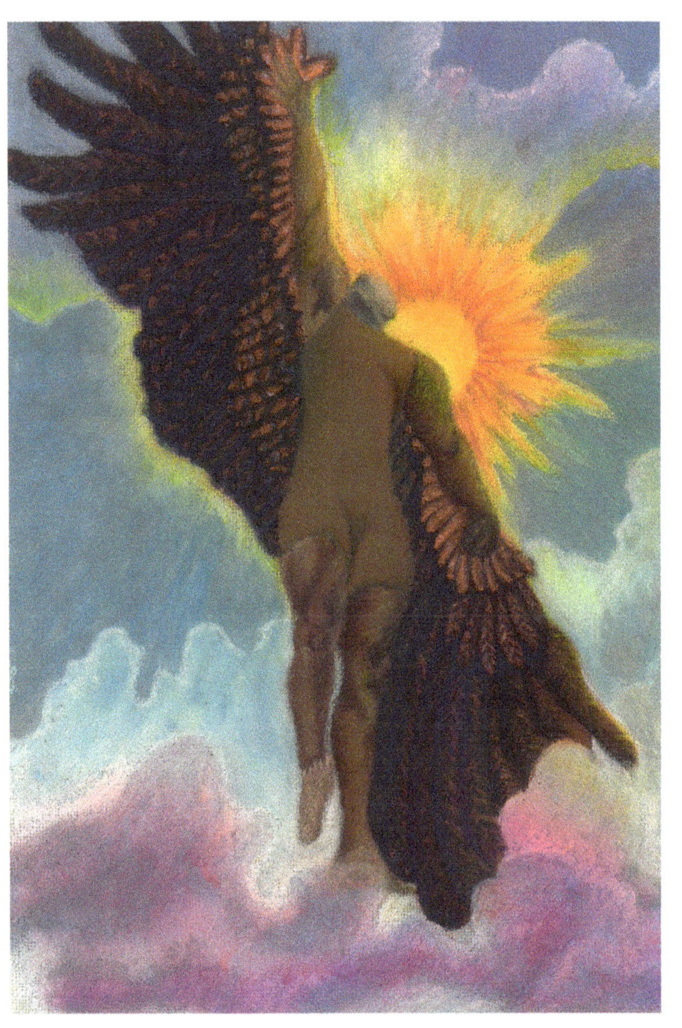

"New Strength—Day"

Isaiah 40:31 (AMP) "But those who wait for the LORD [who expect, look for, and hope in Him] Will gain new strength *and* renew their power; They will lift up their wings [and rise up close to God] like eagles [rising toward the sun]; They will run and not become weary, They will walk and not grow tired."

All of life is a waiting game. We wait to get older, to graduate from high school and college, to get married, to have kids, for the kids to be grown, and, finally, to retire. The only time waiting is worthwhile is when we are waiting on the Lord. As we wait on God, He promises to give us renewed strength. So stop the waiting game and put your hope in the Lord. He will provide you with tools that will help you thrive in your daily walk, and you can also use these tools to help others soar over their problems. God will give you the strength to make it through today, tomorrow, and into eternity.

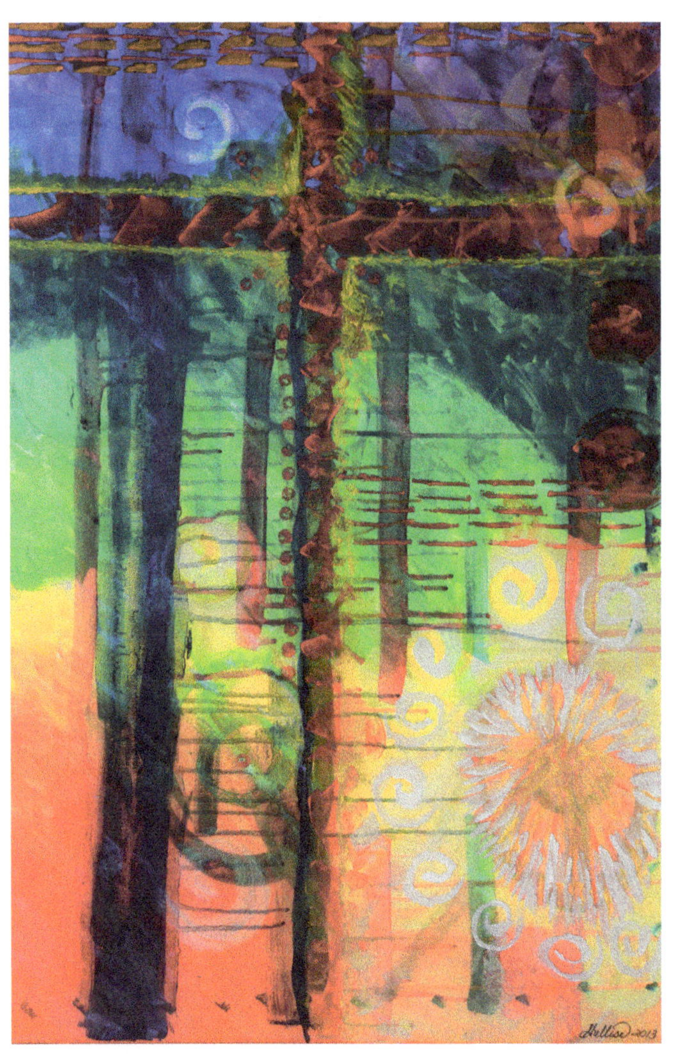

"The Divider of Time"

Luke 23:44-45 (AMP) "It was now about the sixth hour (noon), and darkness came over the whole land until the ninth hour (3:00 p.m.), because the sun was obscured; and the veil [of the Holy of Holies] of the temple was torn in two [from top to bottom]."

We all experience dark times in our lives. Your difficult times may have been as brief as a few days, or you may have endured the darkness for years. During these times, you may experience a variety of emotions. It may seem like your life is at a dead end, with no hope of improvement in sight.

But don't be discouraged. God is with you, even in times of despair. Just hold on. Your future will be brighter. When it seems darkest, be encouraged and know that at a set time, the sun will appear again.

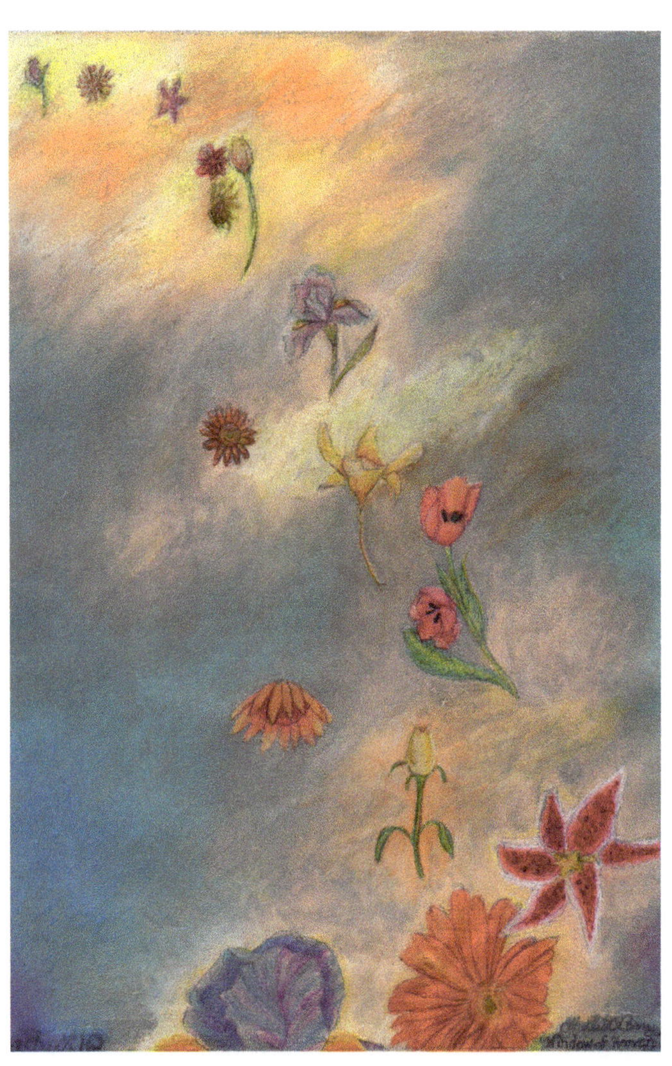

"Windows of Heaven"

Malachi 3:10 (AMP) "'Bring all the tithes (a tenth) into the storehouse, so that there may be food in My house, and test Me now in this,' says the LORD of hosts, 'if I will not open for you the windows of heaven and pour out for you [so great] a blessing until there is no more room to receive it.'"

By giving to your local church, you open yourself up to receive blessings from heaven! These blessings can take on many forms, including finances, good health, a good job, and good relationships. Not only can you give of your finances, but you can also volunteer your time and gifts in service to the Church. Giving opens up the door to receiving more blessings than you can even imagine.

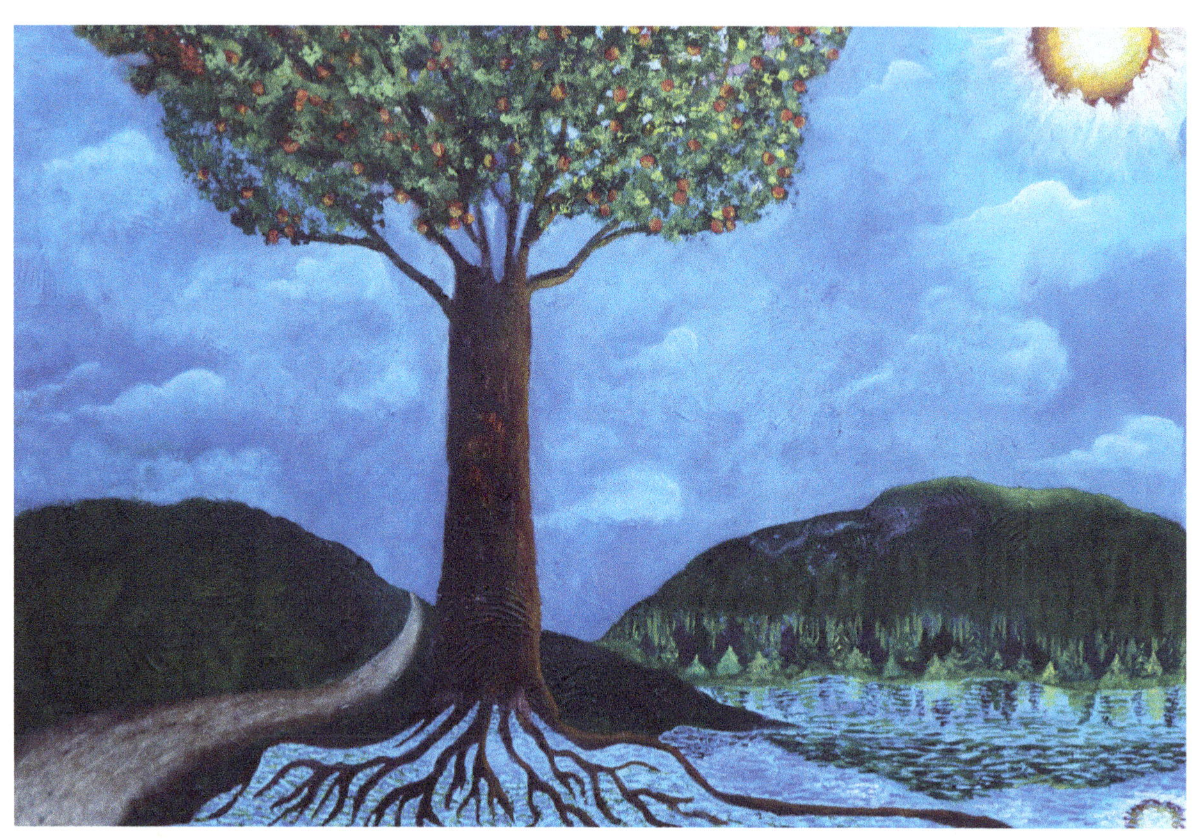

"Prosperous"

Psalms 1:3 (AMP) "And he will be like a tree *firmly* planted [and fed] by streams of water, Which yields its fruit in its season; Its leaf does not wither; And in whatever he does, he prospers [and comes to maturity]."

Everyone wonders about living a prosperous life. Isn't that everyone's goal? But how do we do that? If we keep our focus on the Creator and live by His Word, He promises that whatever we do will prosper. Just as a tree that is planted by the water gets all of the nourishment it needs to become a fruitful tree, we can't help but grow and prosper when we keep our lives rooted in God.

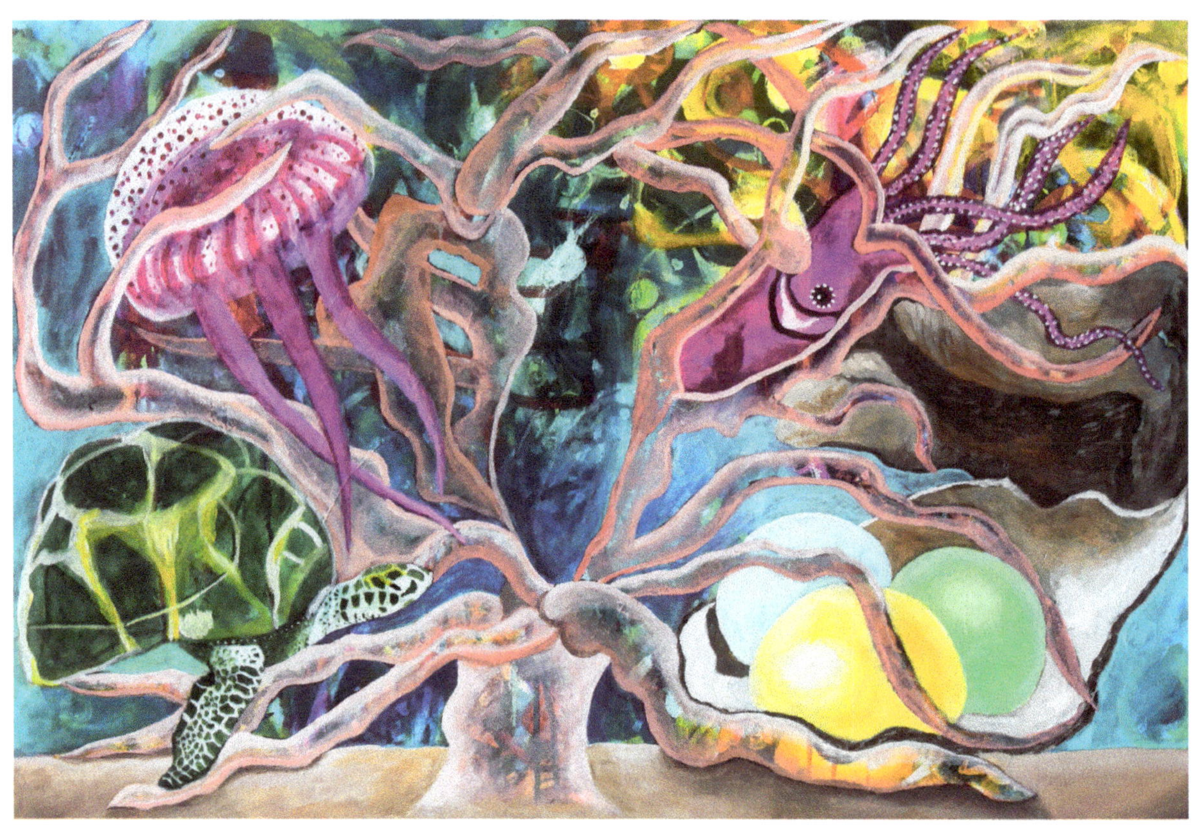

" 5ᵗʰ Day #3 "

Genesis 1:20-21 (AMP) "Then God said, 'Let the waters swarm *and* abundantly produce living creatures, and let birds soar above the earth in the open expanse of the heavens.' God created the great sea monsters and every living creature that moves, with which the waters swarmed according to their kind, and every winged bird according to its kind; and God saw that it was good *and* He affirmed and sustained it."

In the same way that God told the waters to bring forth abundant living creatures, He also wants you to live an abundant life. God sent Jesus into the world to deliver you from sin and to remove the barrier separating you from the Father. Because Jesus died and rose again, you now have direct access to God. In addition, Jesus said that if you stay closely connected to Him, you will produce much fruit (good works for God's Kingdom). Also, you can ask for anything that aligns with God's will, in Jesus' name, and the Father will give it to you. In summary, don't settle for a mundane life when you can live an extraordinary, abundant life with Jesus.

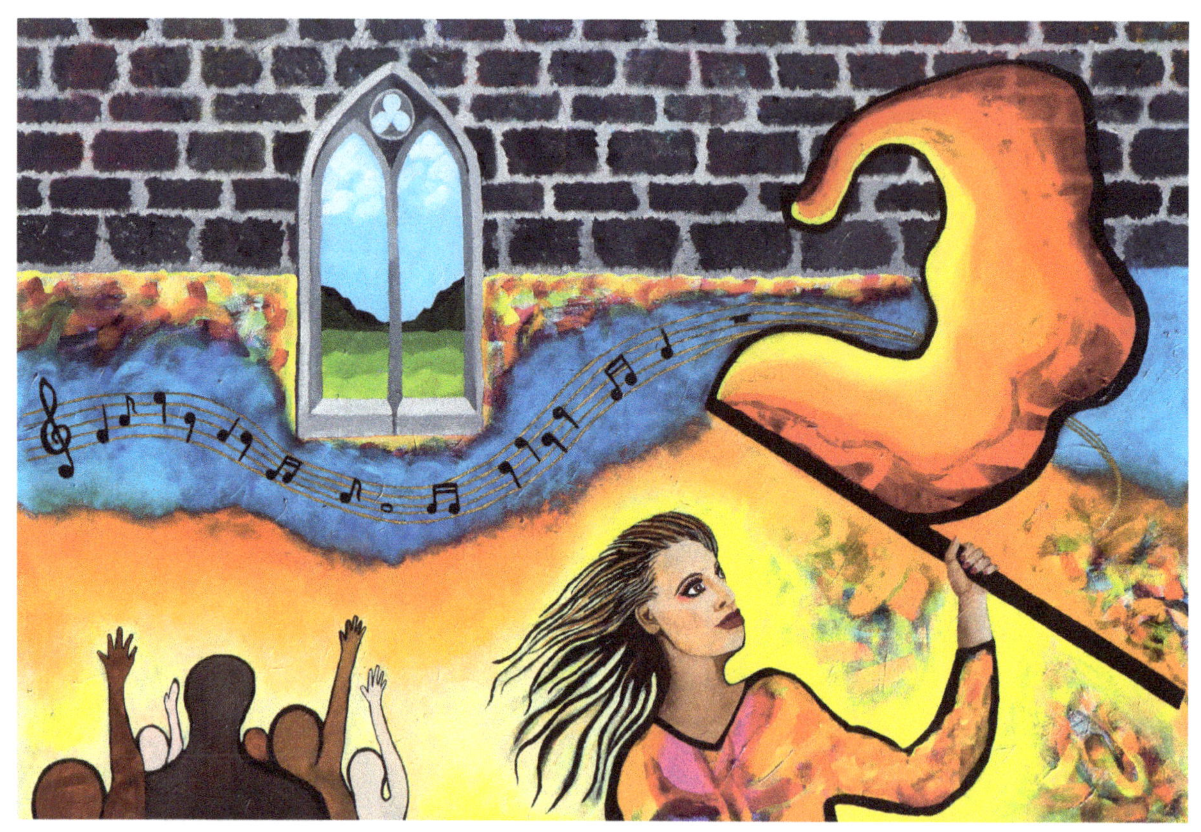

"Praise"

Psalms 146:1-2 (AMP) "Praise the LORD! (Hallelujah!) Praise the LORD, O my soul! While I live I will praise the LORD; I will sing praises to my God as long as I live."

You can tie your thinking into a knot by focusing on things that aren't perfect in your life. It is easy to forget all of the amazing blessings God has given you and all of the miracles God has performed for you. Praising God is a command in the Bible. It will take your focus off your problems when you show gratitude for all He has done for you. Praising Him will help get rid of any feelings of despair, and it's also a good weapon against your enemy, the devil! God is worthy of your praise, and praising Him transports you instantly into His presence. Have you praised Him today?

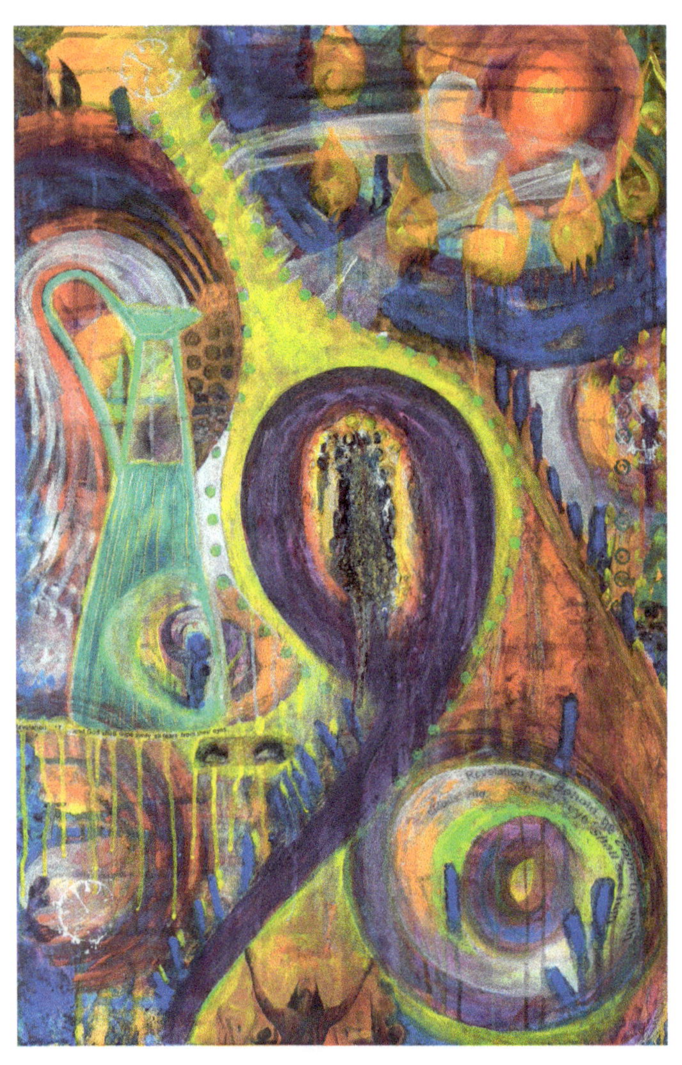

"Behold"

Revelation 1:7 (AMP) "BEHOLD, HE IS COMING WITH THE CLOUDS, **and every eye will see Him…**"

Keep your eyes looking toward heaven, not toward the troubles of life or the despair around you. Know that hope lies ahead of you if you keep your eyes on God. Continue studying and memorizing the Bible as you prepare for Jesus Christ's return to Earth.

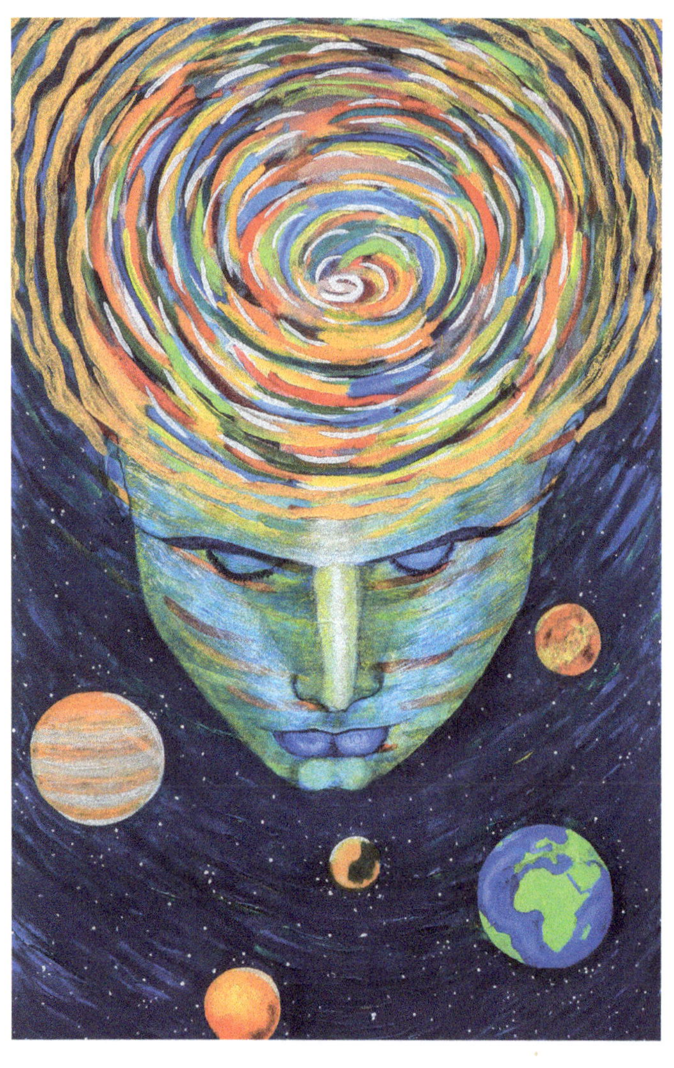

"4th "Day"

Genesis 1:15-16 (AMP) "'…and let them be *useful* as lights in the expanse of the heavens to provide light on the earth'; and it was so, [just as He commanded]. God made the two great lights—the greater light (the sun) to rule the day, and the lesser light (the moon) to rule the night; *He made* the [galaxies of] stars also [that is, all the amazing wonders in the heavens]."

Seven billion eight hundred million! That is how many people are currently in the world.[2] With such a large number of human beings, you may wonder how God can care about you and your needs. You might think He has too many others wanting His attention. You don't have to worry about getting lost in the billions, though.

Psalm 147:4 (AMP) says that God counts the number of stars and calls them all by name. Scientists claim there are one billion trillion stars in the observable universe, which is equal to the number of grains of sand on Earth![3] Surely, He is mindful of you and your needs. So don't worry. He can't forget you. His Word declares that your name is written in the palm of His hand.

---

[2] "World Population Clock," Worldometer, accessed October 27, 2020, https://www.worldometers.info/world-population/.

[3] UCSB Scienceline, accesssed October 27, 2020, http://scienceline.ucsb.edu/getkey.php?key=3775#:~:text=The%20number%20of%20stars%20in,stars%20in%20the%20observable%20universe.

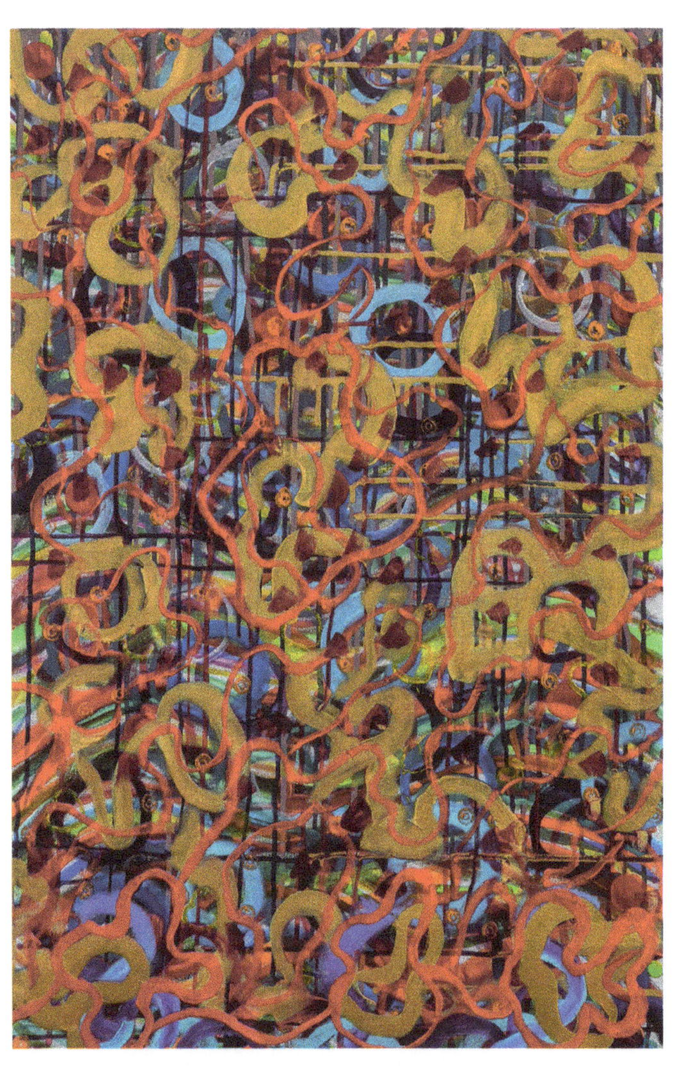

"Greater than Gold"

1 Peter 1:6-7 (NIV) "In all this you greatly rejoice, though now for a little while you may have had to suffer grief in all kinds of trials. These have come so that the proven genuineness of your faith—of greater worth than gold, which perishes even though refined by fire—may result in praise, glory and honor when Jesus Christ is revealed."

You're probably wondering why the difficulties you're facing are necessary. Living the life of a Christian can be compared to the purifying process of gold. Just as gold is put into fire to remove imperfections, you will be tested by various situations. The removal of these impurities will transform you into the likeness of Jesus. When you have been tested, your faith becomes pure and genuine, making it more valuable than gold.

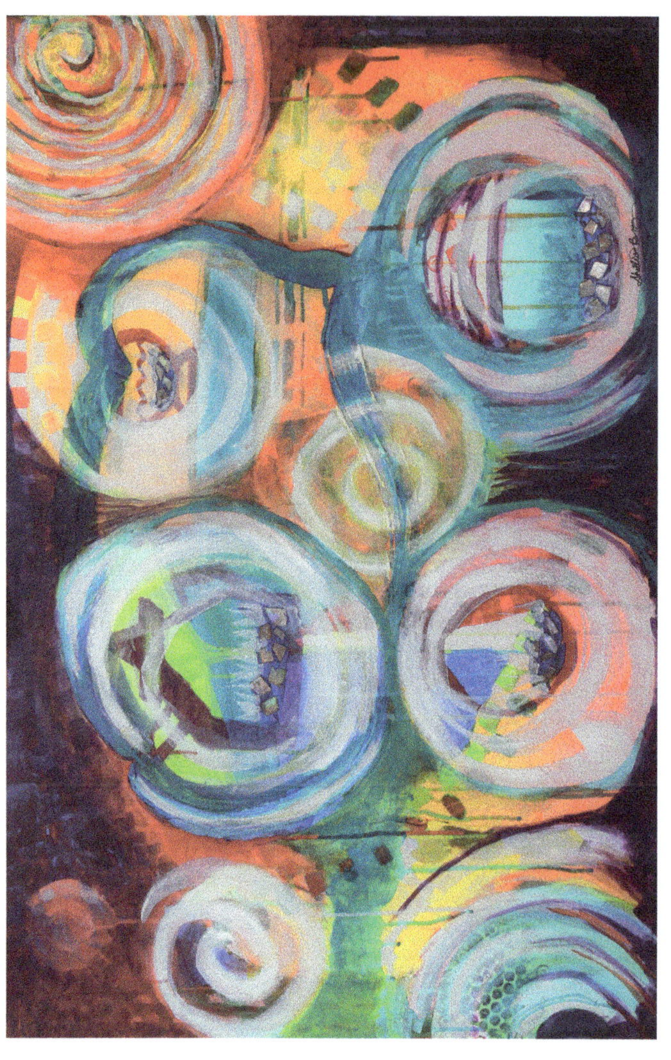

"Tree of Life"

"Proverbs 15:4 (AMP) "A soothing tongue [speaking words that build up and encourage] is a tree of life, But a perversive tongue [speaking words that overwhelm and depress] crushes the spirit."

Just as true spiritual nourishment comes from above and is uplifting, we are to use our words to inspire those that we encounter. Words can be used in a positive or negative manner. You should use your words for the encouragement and healing of others. But often, we use our words to tear down and harm.

Let's use Christian pastor Greg Laurie's acronym for thinking before we speak. Ask yourself these questions:

T- Is it Truthful?

H- Is it Helpful?

I- Is it Inspiring?

N- Is it Necessary?

K- Is it Kind?[4]

Test your words using the "THINK" acronym, and your words will never fail to be a blessing to others.

[4] Greg Laurie, "T.H.I.N.K.!!!", accessed October 27, 2020, https://harvest.org/resources/gregs-blog/post/t-h-i-n-k/.

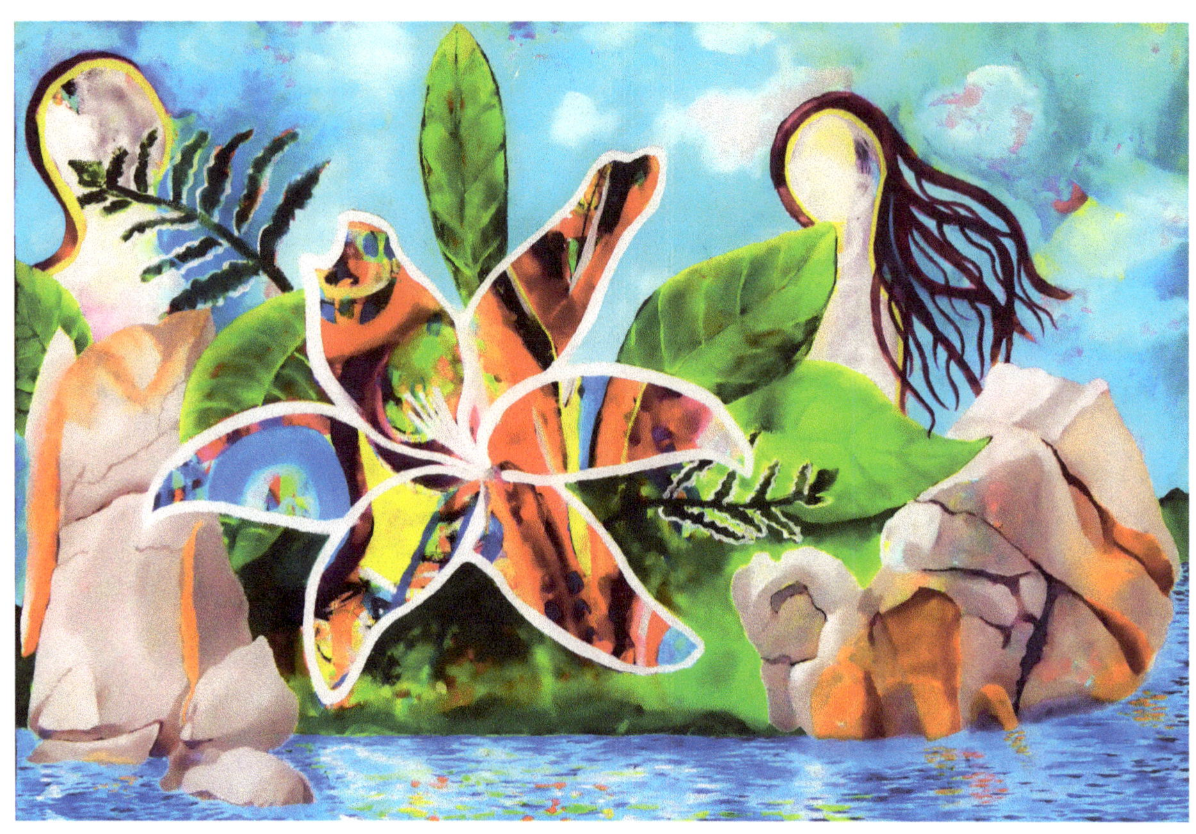

"In the Cool of the Day"

Genesis 3:8 (AMP) "And they heard the sound of the Lord God walking in the garden in the cool [afternoon breeze] of the day, so the man and his wife hid *and* kept themselves hidden from the presence of the Lord God among the trees of the garden."

God desires to spend time with you, His masterpiece. As a part of His great creation, He has blessed us with the gift of free will. We have all made decisions we wish we could change. Some of these decisions may have made you feel unworthy of His love. Isn't it wonderful to know God loves you no matter the choices you have made? And those choices can't separate you from His love. He's waiting to erase those negative experiences and welcome you into His open arms. God is longing to spend time with you.

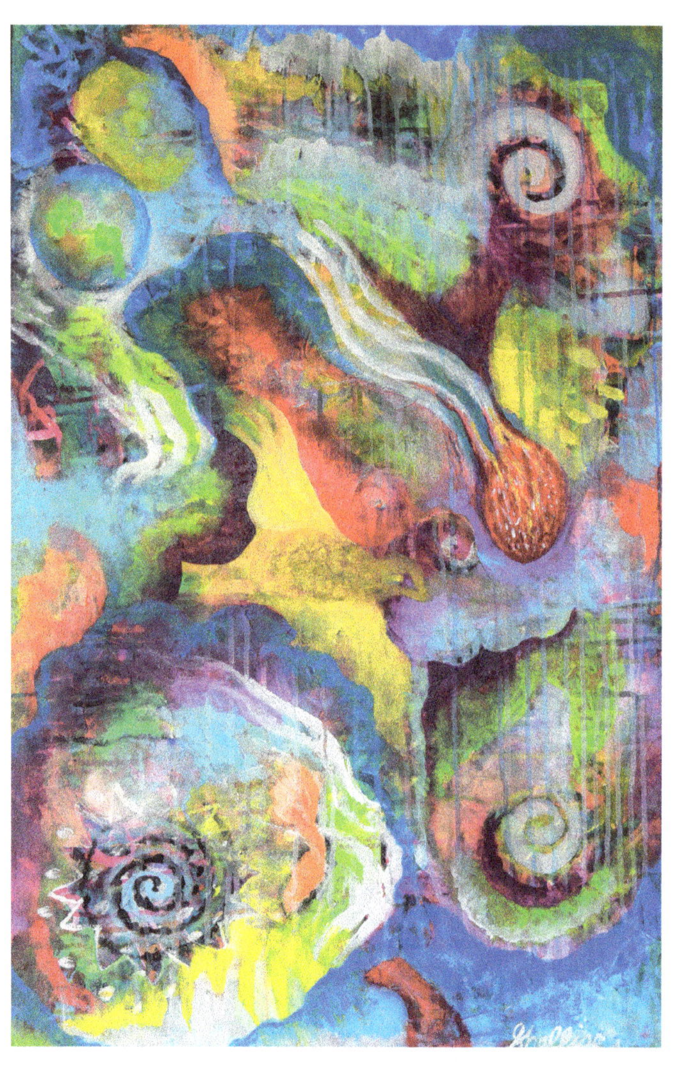

"Glory"

Psalms 19:1 (AMP) "The heavens are telling of the glory of God; And the expanse [of heaven] is declaring the work of His hands."

The heavens are magnificent! There are so many galaxies yet to be discovered! You don't have to look far to notice the glory of God. You can find it in the stars and constellations. God made the stars on the fourth day of Creation and set them in the sky to light your way in the darkness. The stars were designed to lead you to the Creator and to reveal His greatness! When was the last time you stood in awe as you gazed upon the night sky? Go out tonight, take a look, and enjoy His presence!

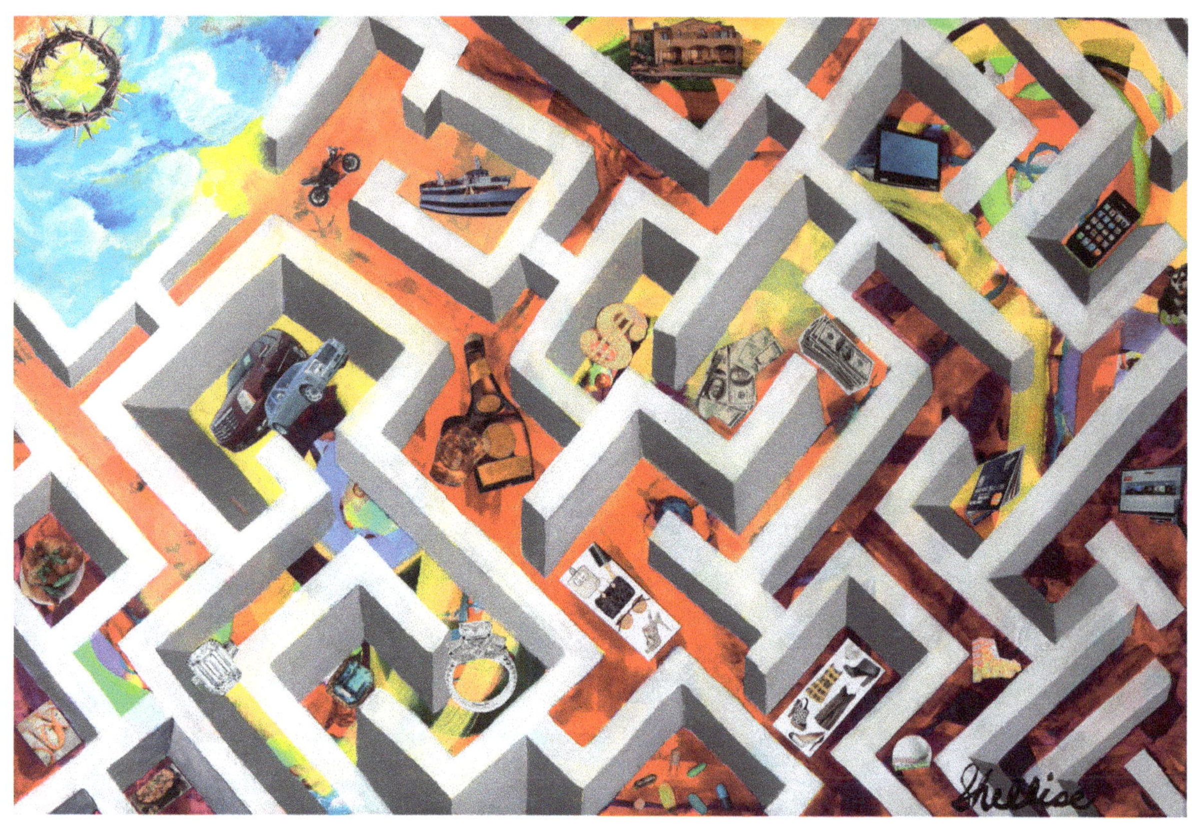

"The Maze of Life"

John 14:6 (AMP) "Jesus said to him, 'I am the [only] Way [to God] and the [real] Truth and the [real] Life; no one comes to the Father but through Me.'"

Advertisers and the media would have you believe that you can't be happy or satisfied without the largest house, the newest car, or the finest clothes. In life, there are many paths that lead to temporary satisfaction, but these passing pleasures lead us away from the Creator. The American dream has become a quest for more and more things, and it usually ends in debt, a fate almost worse than death! Debt is a trap of the devil. It is a way for him to steal your joy. He keeps your resources tied up, preventing them from being used to grow God's Kingdom. There is only one true path that leads to everlasting peace, and Jesus is the way.

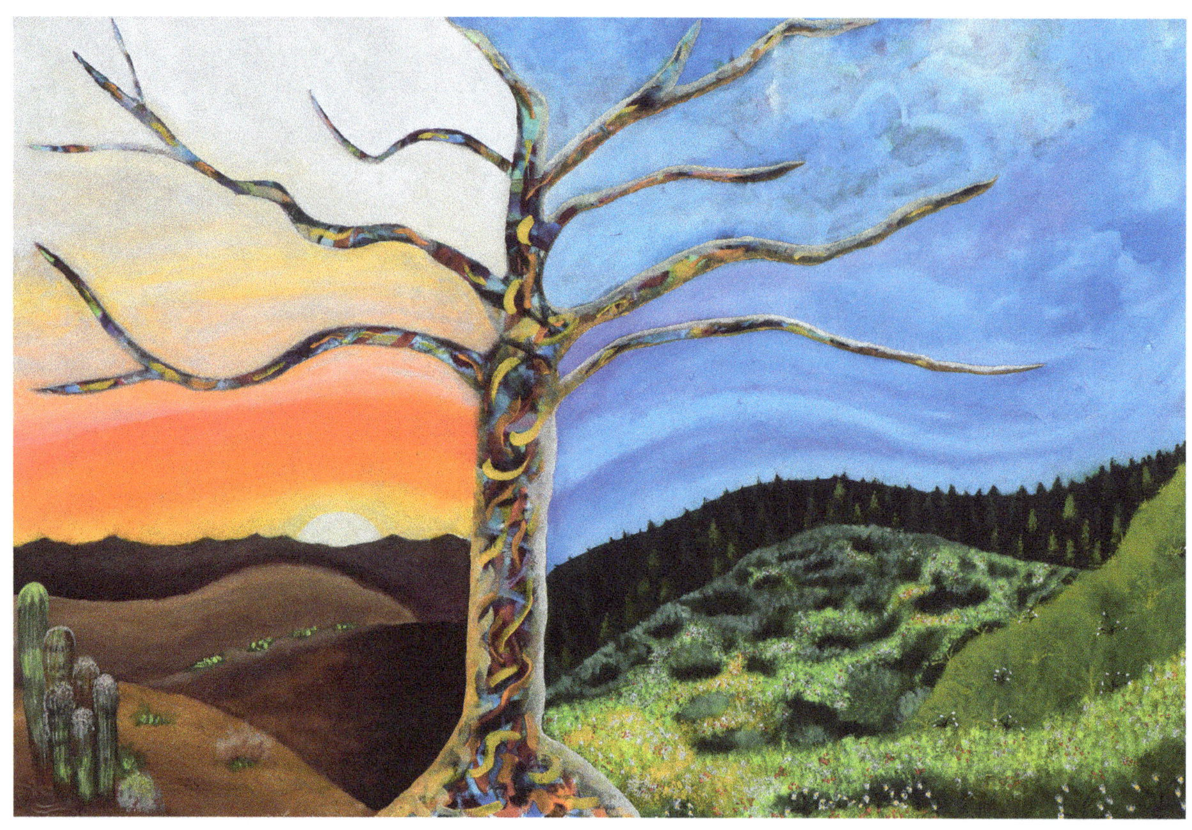

"Hope"

Isaiah 35:1-4 (AMP) "The wilderness and the dry land will be glad; The Arabah (desert) will shout in exultation and blossom Like the autumn crocus. It will blossom abundantly And rejoice with joy and singing. The glory of Lebanon will be given to it, The majesty of [Mount] Carmel and [the plain] of Sharon. They will see the glory of the Lord, The majesty *and* splendor of our God. Encourage the exhausted, and make staggering knees firm. Say to those with an anxious *and* panic-stricken heart, 'Be strong, fear not! Indeed, your God will come with vengeance [for the ungodly]; The retribution of God will come, But He will save you.'"

Are you feeling anxious and full of despair because you are currently in a desert season of your life? There is hope, even when you're going through your desert, because God is still by your side. So be encouraged, for the Bible says He will never leave or abandon you. In the Lord's perfect timing, He will turn your desert into blossoming landscapes and fill you with an abundance of hope and joy.

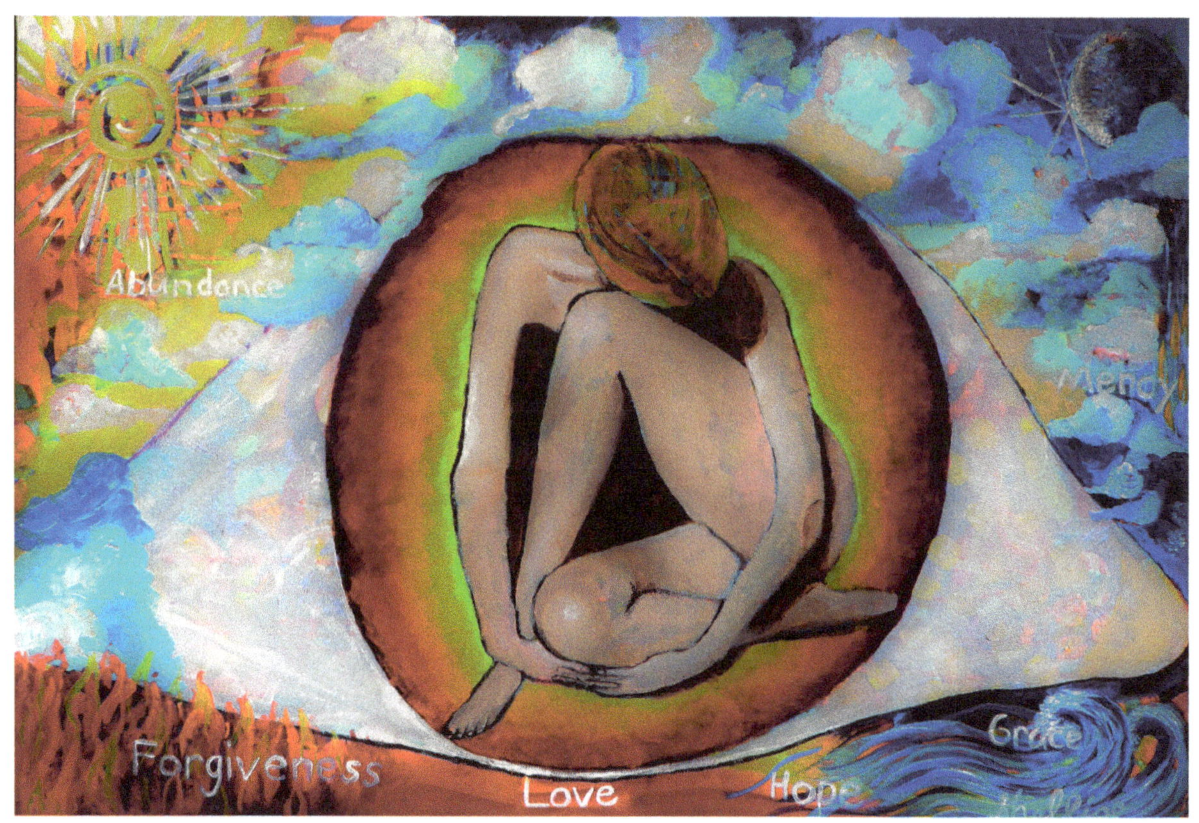

"His Eye"

Psalms 139:7-10 (AMP) "Where can I go from Your Spirit? Or where can I flee from Your presence? If I ascend to heaven, You are there; If I make my bed in Sheol (the nether world, the place of the dead), behold, You are there. If I take the wings of the dawn, If I dwell in the remotest part of the sea, Even there Your hand will lead me, And Your right hand will take hold of me."

Has God been trying to get your attention? Have you been running and hiding from Him? Did He tell you to go to a specific place to carry out His will? Or maybe God has given you an exact set of instructions that sound nearly impossible. God specializes in the impossible! In Psalm 139:7-10, David writes how futile it is to run from God. Do you feel you have made a mess of your life? God sees you no matter the state of your soul, and He still wants to use you for His Kingdom. There is nowhere you can hide from His love.

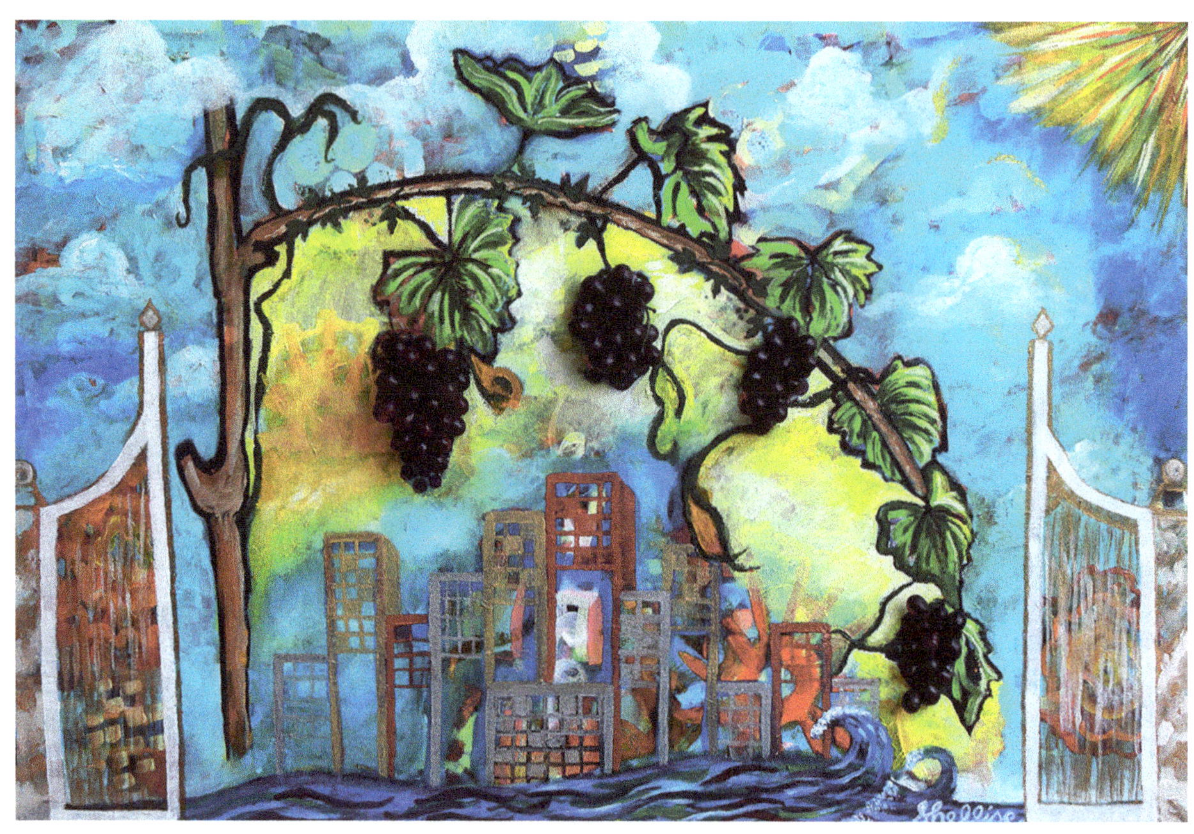

"Treasures"

Matthew 6:20-21 (AMP) "'But store up for yourselves treasures in heaven, where neither moth nor rust destroys, and where thieves do not break in and steal; for where your treasure is, there your heart [your wishes, your desires; that on which your life centers] will be also.'"

Did you know that you can build up treasures in heaven that will be waiting for you when you arrive? Those treasures are created by the works you do for the Lord here on Earth. The Bible says that only the work you do for Jesus will last into eternity. The material possessions that you gather and store during your earthly life will not matter in the scope of eternity. Those things will all burn in the end. The old proverb "You can't take it with you" is only partially true. Now you can start sending your treasures to your eternal home.

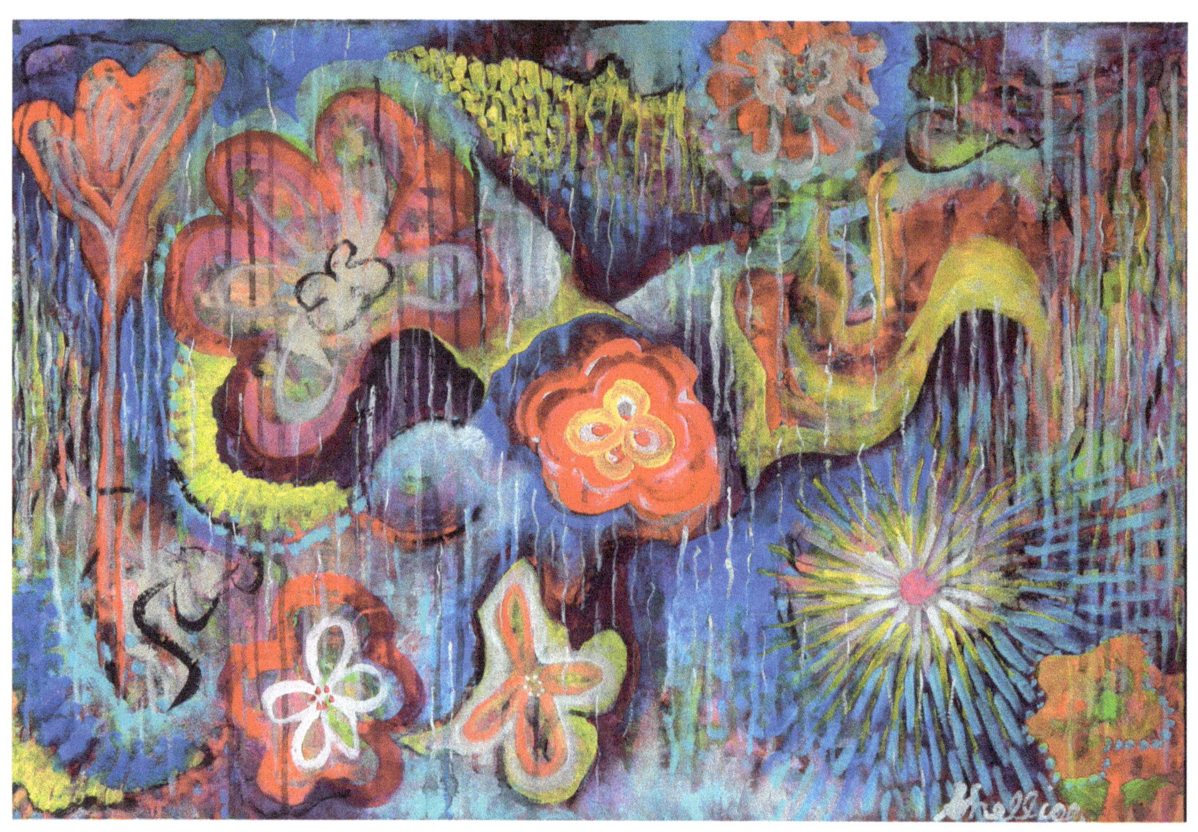

"Rain"

Deuteronomy 28:12 (AMP) "'The Lord will open for you His good treasure house, the heavens, to give rain to your land in its season and to bless all the work of your hand...'"

As we accept, follow, and obey our Creator, He will provide the rain, in the form of blessings, that you need in order to flourish in all seasons of your life. God is omniscient! He knows everything about you and your needs, wants, and desires. If you listen diligently and pay respectful attention to the Bible, He will gladly rain down blessings on everything you do.

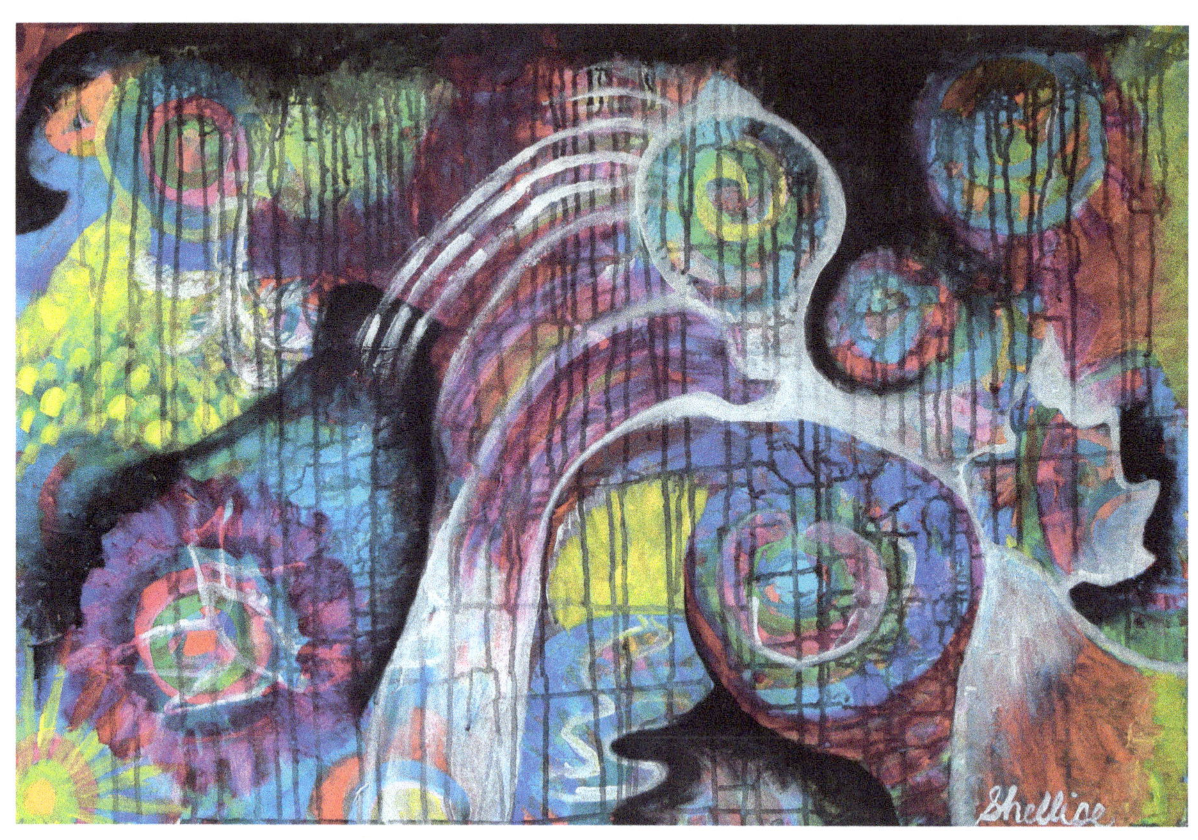

"Fear no Evil"

Psalm 23:4 (AMP) "Even though I walk through the [sunless] valley of the shadow of death, I fear no evil, for You are with me…"

The problems and dangers of this world are worse than they have ever been in the history of mankind. The circumstances of life may have placed you in a dark valley. Maybe it's a wayward child, the loss of a job, or bad news from your doctor. You don't have to be afraid while you travel through the valley. You may feel like you are alone in the darkness, but God is with you and will never leave you. He will provide the light and strength you need in order to overcome your trials and ascend to the mountaintop.

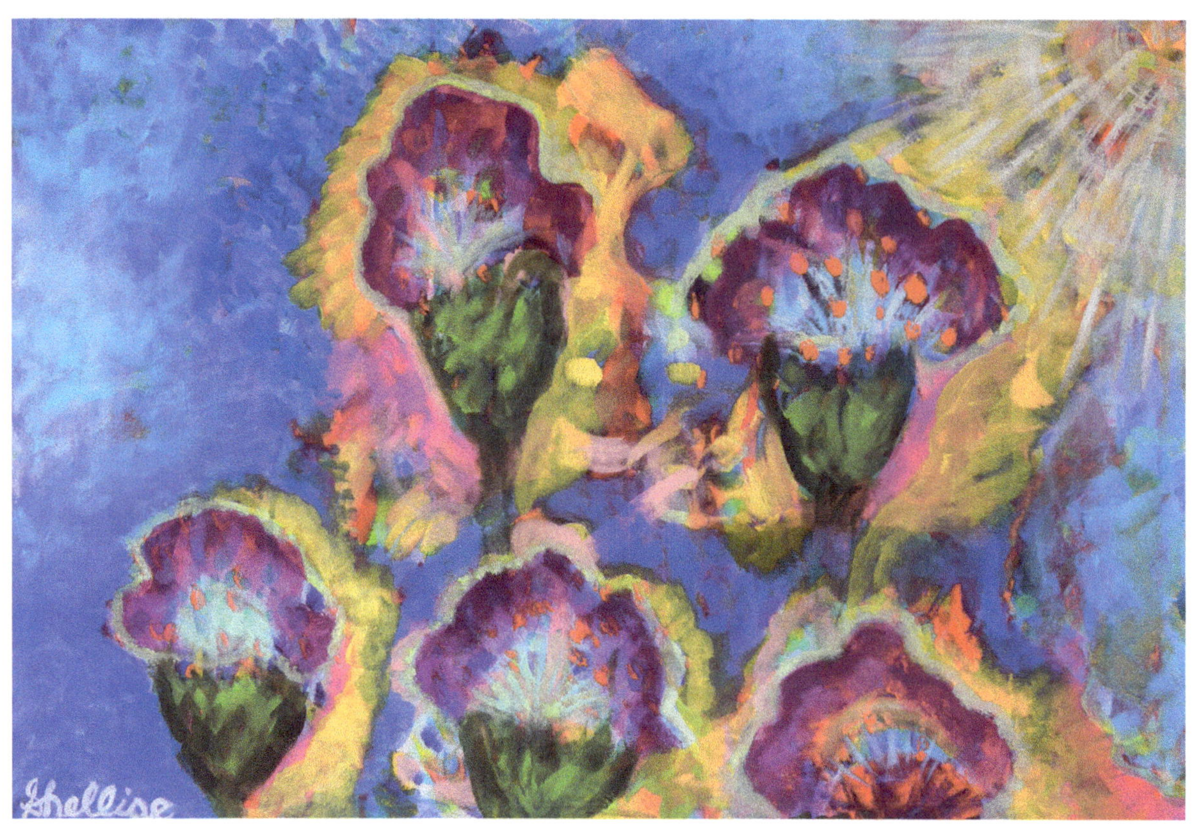

"Don't Worry"

Luke 12:27-28 (AMP) "'Consider the lilies *and* wildflowers, how they grow [in the open field]. They neither labor nor spin [wool to make clothing]; yet I tell you, not even Solomon in all his glory *and* splendor dressed himself like one of these. But if this is how God clothes the grass which is in the field today and tomorrow is thrown into the furnace, how much more *will He clothe* you? You of little faith!'"

God delicately formed your body. It wasn't built to withstand large amounts of stress. He never intended for you to worry every day about what you will need to survive. Even in your darkest times, you can find encouragement by looking at how our Lord provides for all of His creations every day. Flowers don't have to labor to grow. It happens effortlessly because the Lord made them that way. Give your body a rest today. Surrender your worries to the Lord. He will supply all your needs. God will never fail you.

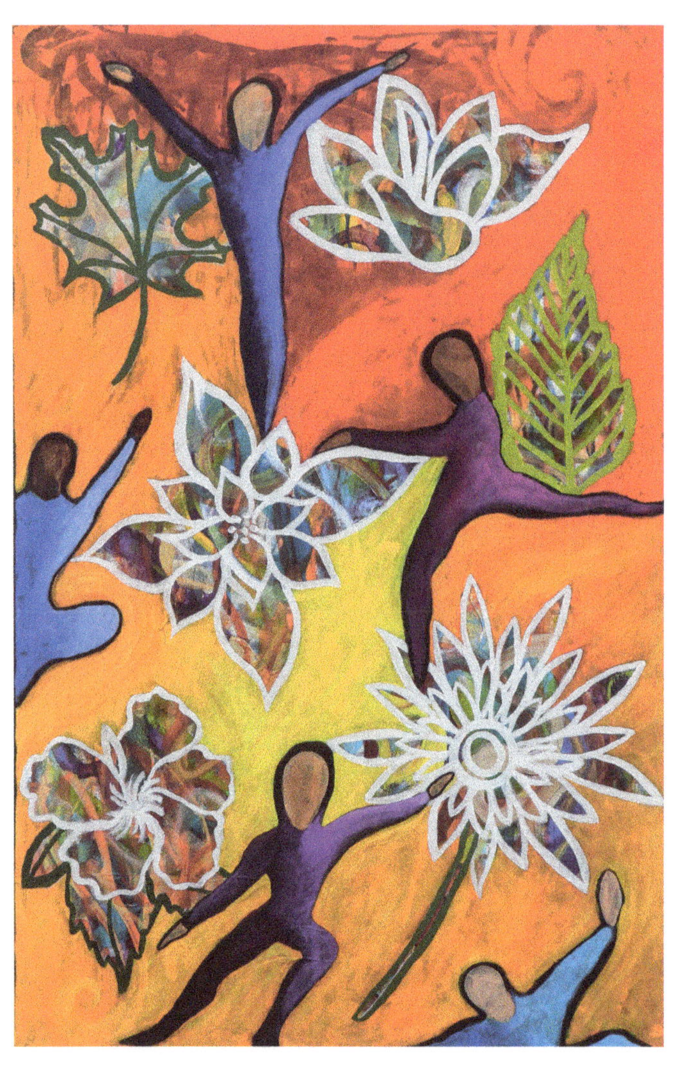

"In His Time"

Ecclesiastes 3:1-4 (AMP) "There is a season (a time appointed) for everything and a time for every delight *and* event *or* purpose under heaven— A time to be born and a time to die; A time to plant and a time to uproot what is planted. A time to kill and a time to heal; A time to tear down and a time to build up. A time to weep and a time to laugh; A time to mourn and a time to dance."

Are you waiting for God to deliver you from your trial, to reveal His purpose for your life, or to give you the green light to start your ministry? Often, God's timing will not match the timing you desire. If you're like everyone else on Earth, you probably want God to answer your prayers right away. The Bible says there is an appointed time for everything under heaven. Just remember, God's timing is always perfect, even when it feels slow. You can trust in His schedule. Rest assured that He will never be a second late.

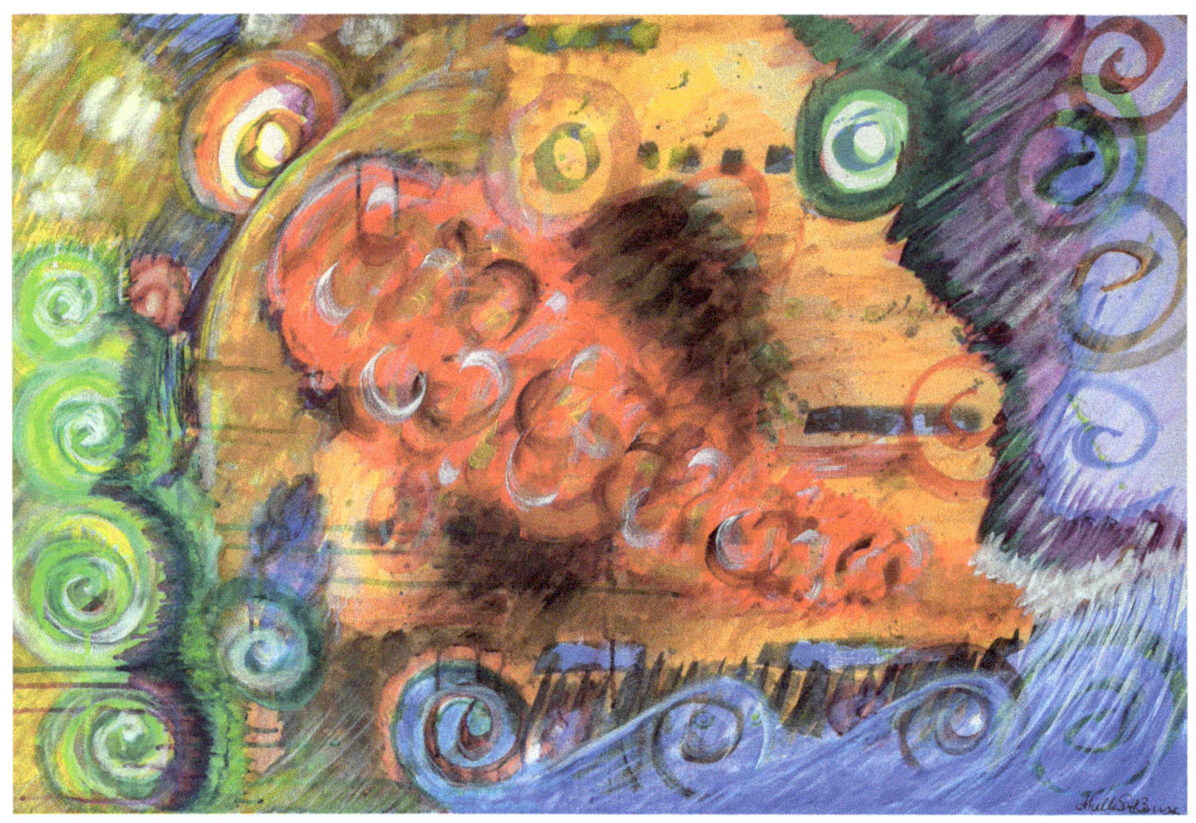

"Elements"

1 Kings 19:3, 7-8 (AMP) "And Elijah was afraid and arose and ran for his life, and he came to Beersheba which belongs to Judah, and he left his servant there."

"Then the angel of the Lord came again a second time and touched him and said, 'Get up, and eat, for the journey is too long for you [without adequate sustenance].' So he got up and ate and drank, and with the strength of that food he traveled forty days and nights to Horeb (Sinai), the mountain of God."

It may seem like you're under attack on all sides. You may feel trapped in a corner by the situation in your life. Things may appear hopeless, and maybe you're ready to give up. But hold on. God will supply a solution to your problems. He is the God who provides. He has the answer even before you form the question. He will give you the necessary strength to move forward and complete the life task that He designed for you long before you were born. Just Hold On!

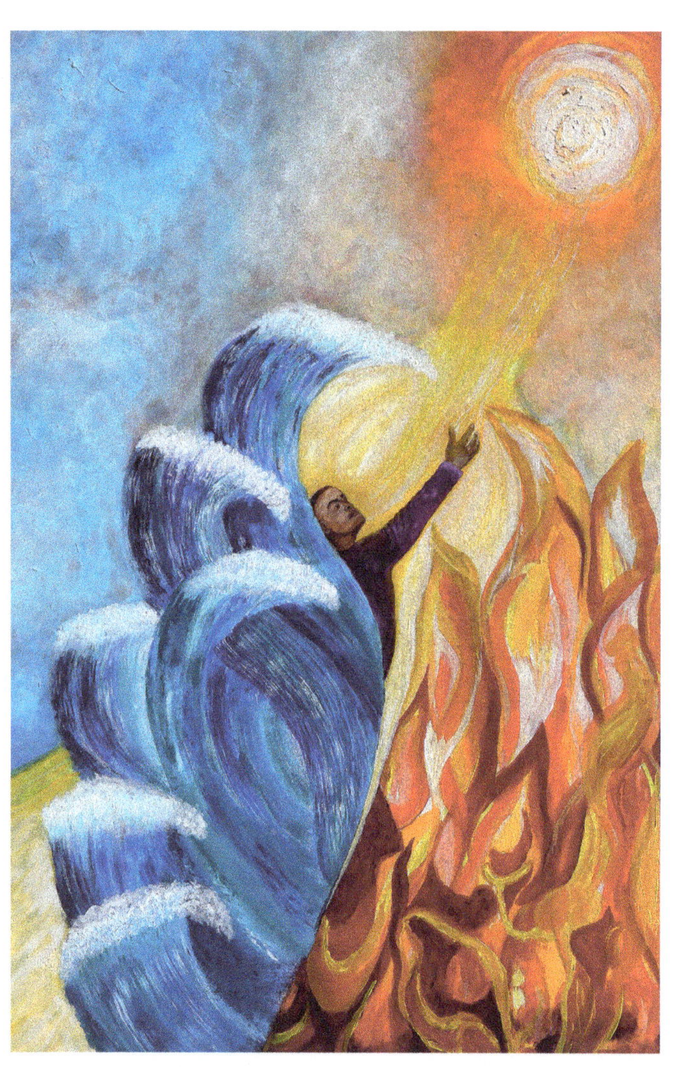

"Untouchable"

Isaiah 43:2 (AMP) "'When you pass through the waters, I will be with you; And through the rivers, they will not overwhelm you. When you walk through fire, you will not be scorched, Nor will the flame burn you.'"

Did you know that once you become a child of God, He has you under His protection? No matter the severity or size of the circumstance you are facing, God has everything under control. Even when your situation appears to be impossible to resolve, He won't let those problems overwhelm you. The conflicts of your life don't catch God off guard. He is always aware of the struggles you face. So don't worry. Put your faith and trust in God. Remember, you're under His protection.

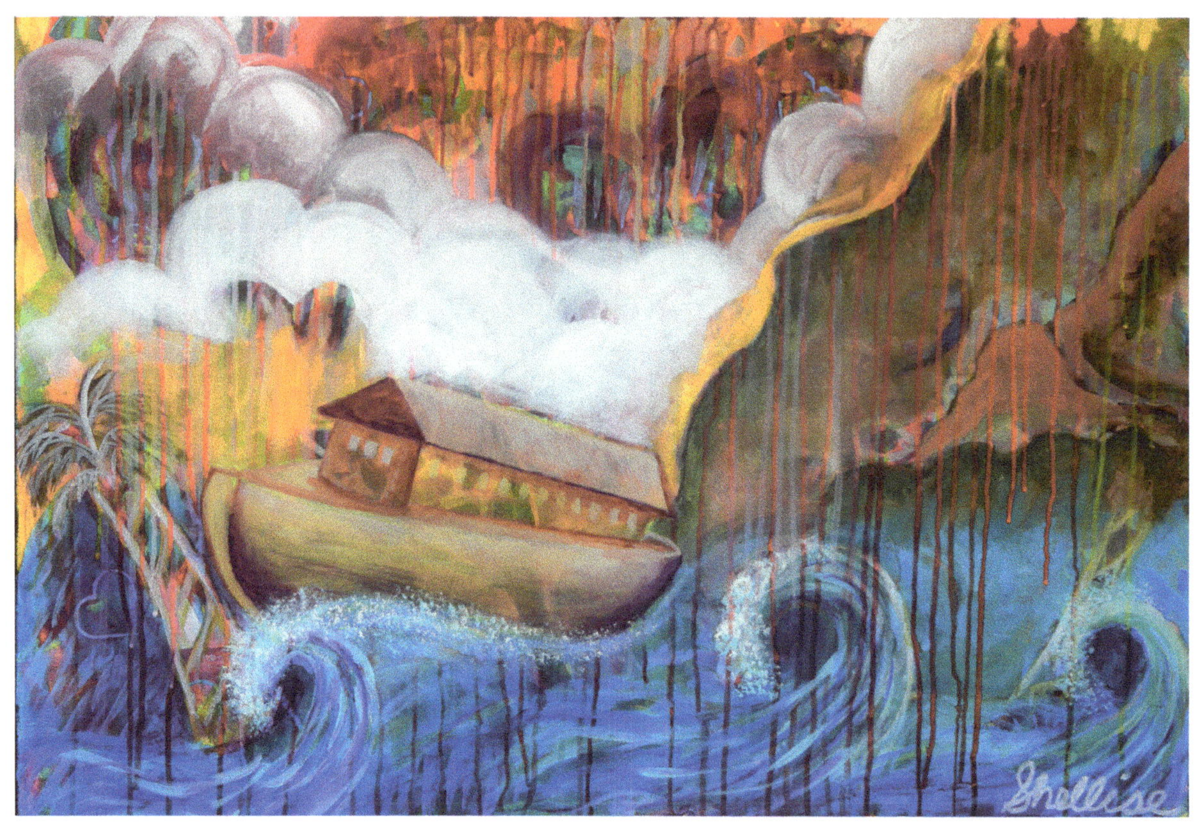

"The Flood"

Genesis 7:15-17 (AMP) "So they went into the ark with Noah, two by two of all living beings in which there was the breath *and* spirit of life. Those which entered, male and female of all flesh (creatures), entered as God had commanded Noah; and the LORD closed *the door* behind him. The flood [the great downpour of rain] was forty days *and* nights on the earth; and the waters increased and lifted up the ark and it floated [high] above the land."

As a believer moving through life, there will be many tests and trials you will encounter. You don't have to worry about the outcome, because God said in His Word that He would never leave you or forsake you. He will walk by your side through the storms of life and provide the protection that you will need. You can proceed confidently through life knowing that at the appropriate time, God will raise you above the storm.

"Winds and Sea Obey"

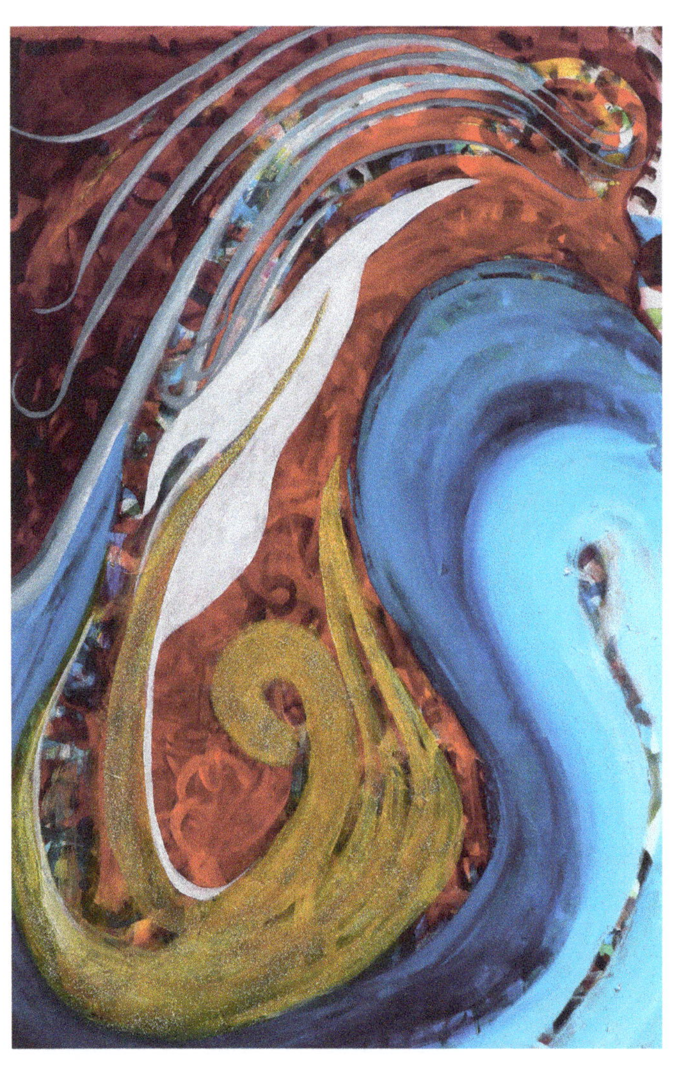

Matthew 8:23-27 (AMP) "When He got into the boat, His disciples followed Him. And suddenly a violent storm arose on the sea, so that the boat was being covered by the waves; but Jesus was sleeping. And the disciples went and woke Him, saying, 'Lord, save us, we are going to die!' He said to them, 'Why are you afraid, you men of little faith?' Then He got up and rebuked the winds and the sea, and there was [at once] a great and wonderful calm [a perfect peacefulness]. The men wondered in amazement, saying, 'What kind of man is this, that even the winds and the sea obey Him?'"

Your current circumstances may have you in a position that seems impossible to resolve. You're probably wondering if God will be able to fix the situation you're in. Maybe your choices have put you in this crisis, or maybe it's a test or trial from God. No matter how you got into this predicament, God is able to work it out for the good and betterment of His Kingdom. Nothing is impossible for God. Since Jesus was able to command the winds and sea and they obeyed Him, He can produce the same results in your life. So, surrender your troubles to Jesus. He will calm the storms of your life.

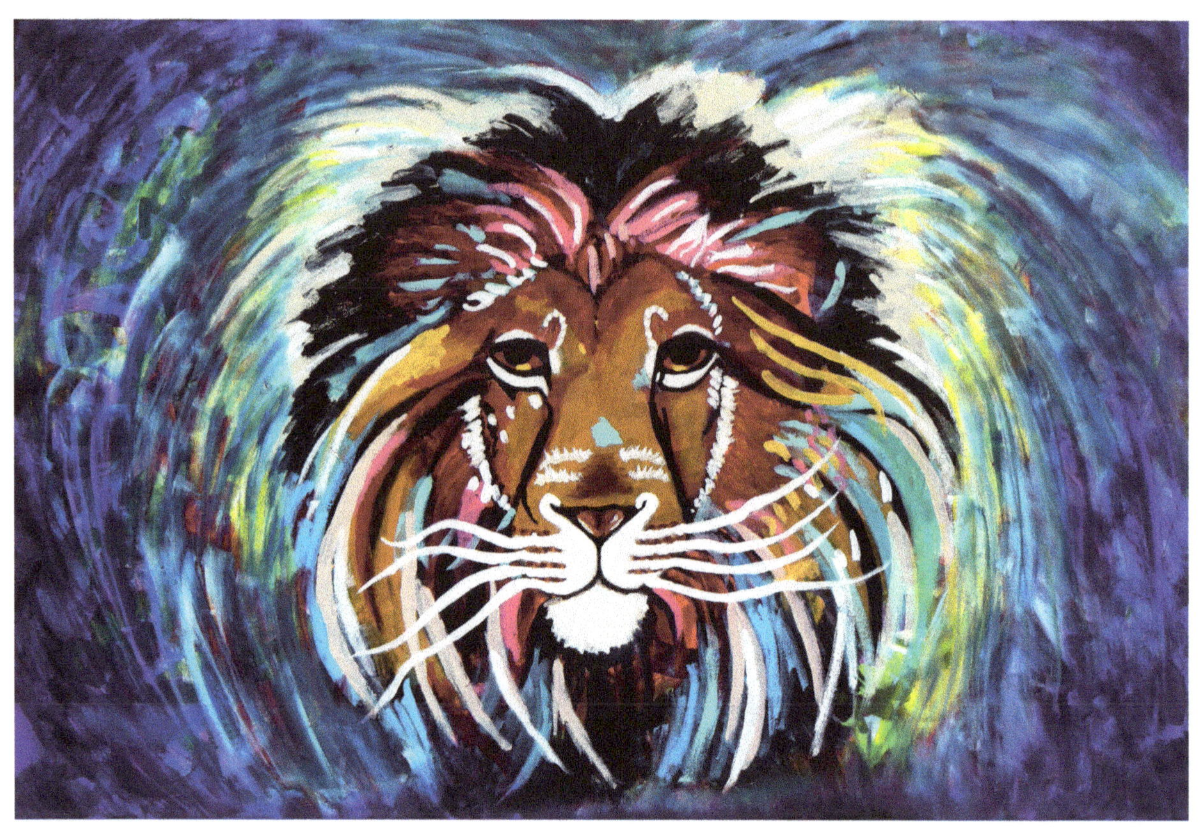

"Bold"

Proverbs 28:1 (AMP) "The wicked flee when no one pursues them, But the righteous are as bold as a lion."

Many of us spend our time walking through life in fear. Fear of failure, of measuring up, and even of success. You don't have to live in fear. All of the gifts and talents you need in order to become the best you can be are already within you. They have been given to you by the Creator. Develop your talents into skills so you can become the person you are meant to be: fearless, unafraid, and BOLD!

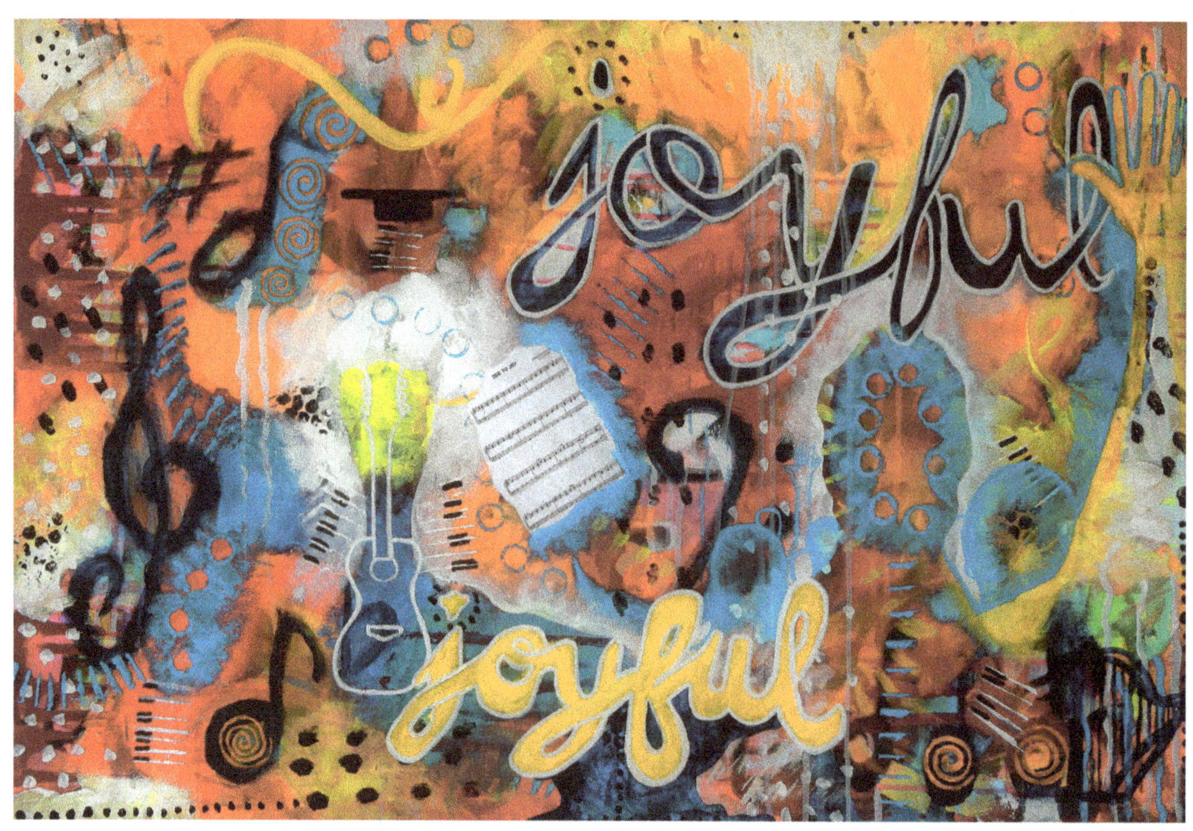

"Joyful Noise"

Psalm 95:1-3 (KJV) "O come, let us sing unto the LORD: let us make a joyful noise to the rock of our salvation. Let us come before his presence with thanksgiving, and make a joyful noise unto him with psalms. For the LORD is a great God, and a great King above all gods."

Do you find yourself flooded with negative emotions because of the problems you are facing? These circumstances may have left you feeling hopeless. Are you looking for a solution to pull you out of the pit of despair? Music has the ability to lift you up from those dark places. Make a joyful noise by singing praises to God. The Bible states seven times to make a joyful noise. You can sing or play an instrument in honor of God. As you sing, remember all He has done for you. Sing of His unending goodness, mercy, grace, and love.

So, the next time you're feeling down, sing a song and make a joyful noise. You'll feel so much better that you'll be amazed!

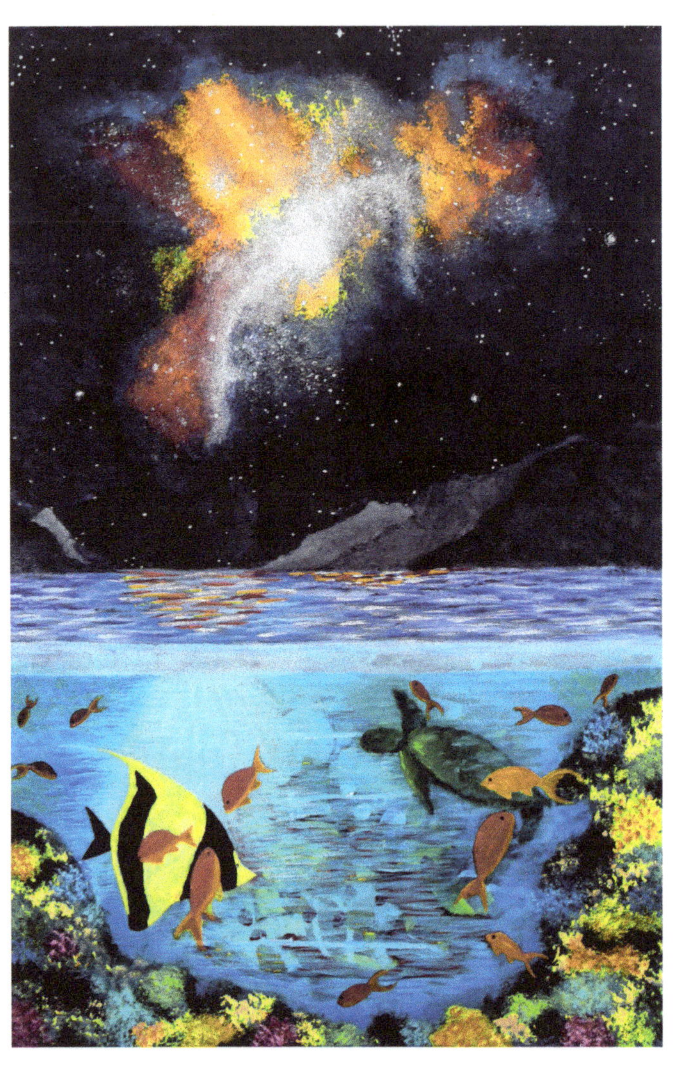

"Limitless Love"

Romans 8:38-39 (AMP) "For I am convinced [and continue to be convinced—beyond any doubt] that neither death, nor life, nor angels, nor principalities, nor things present *and* threatening, nor things to come, nor power, nor height, nor depth, nor any other created thing, will be able to separate us from the [unlimited] love of God, which is in Christ Jesus our Lord."

Before God formed you, He loved you. Before you were born, He claimed you as His own. Even at birth, God had already appointed you to accomplish great things as an ambassador of His Kingdom. Isn't it amazing that He chose to love you before you knew He existed? He knew all of the decisions you would make in life, but He was determined to send His only begotten Son, Jesus, to pay the ultimate price for your freedom. Can you imagine how much He loves you? His love for you is infinite, never-ending, and limitless.

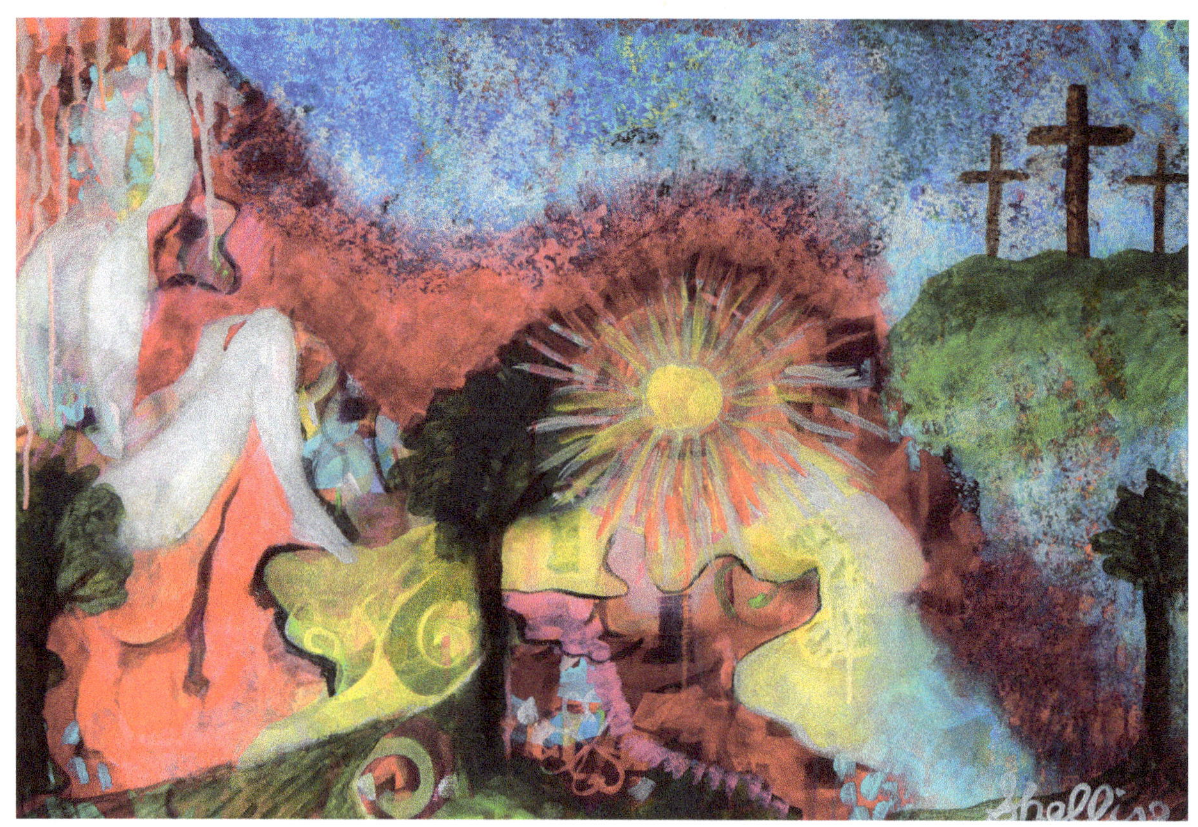

"Resurrection"

Matthew 28:5-7 (AMP) "But the angel said to the women, 'Do not be afraid; for I know that you are looking for Jesus who has been crucified. He is not here, for He has risen, just as He said [He would]. Come! See the place where He was lying. Then go quickly and tell His disciples that He has risen from the dead; and behold, He is going ahead of you into Galilee [as He promised]. There you will see Him; behold, I have told you.'"

God always keeps His word. Jesus told His disciples that He would suffer, die, and rise again on the third day, and He did! The women were the first witnesses of the empty tomb. They gladly followed the angel's instructions and ran back to Galilee to share the good news with the disciples. Has God spoken to you about the work He wants you to do for His Kingdom? His promises are true. You just need to take the first step toward your destiny.

"Promise"

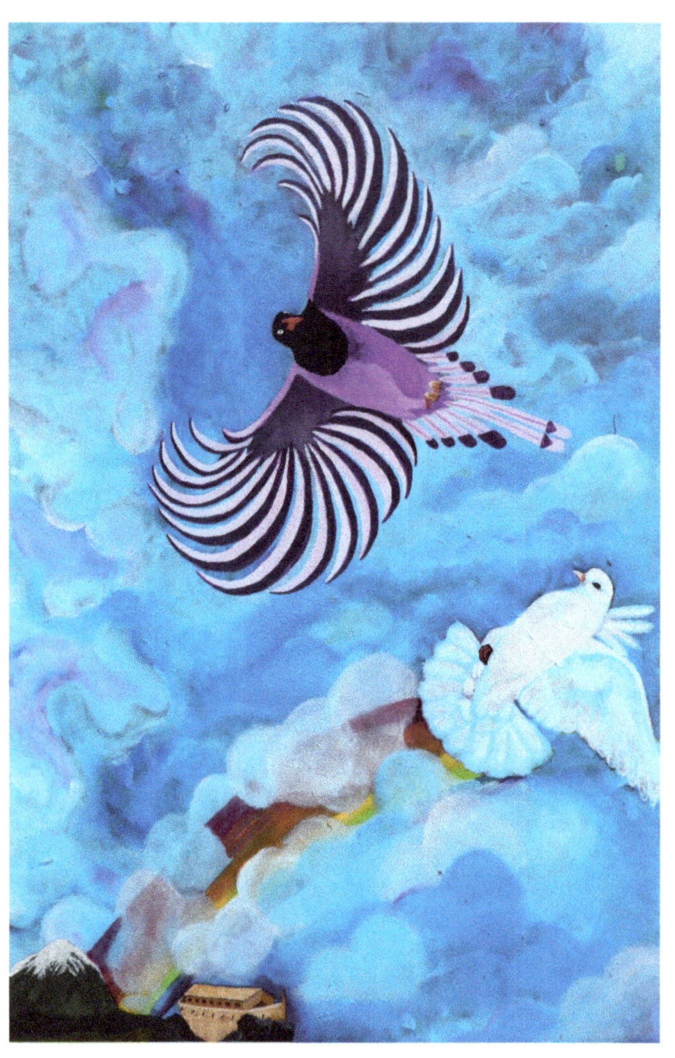

Genesis 9:11-13 (AMP) "'I will establish My covenant with you: Never again shall all flesh be cut off by the water of a flood, nor shall there ever again be a flood to destroy *and* ruin the earth.' And God said, 'This is the token (visible symbol, memorial) of the [solemn] covenant which I am making between Me and you and every living creature that is with you, for all future generations; I set My rainbow in the clouds, and it shall be a sign of a covenant between Me and the earth.'"

How many people have broken their word to you in your lifetime? You could probably name a few people, or maybe there have been too many to count. There is one person who will never break a promise to you, and that is God. He always keeps His word, and His word produces what He intends.

After the great flood, God promised Noah that He would never destroy the earth again with a flood. As a token of His promise, God placed the first rainbow in the sky.

So, on your rainy days, when you feel as though there is no one you can trust, look up at the partially sunny sky. You will find God's rainbow. It will be there to remind you that there is always someone who will be there for you. You can rely on Him.

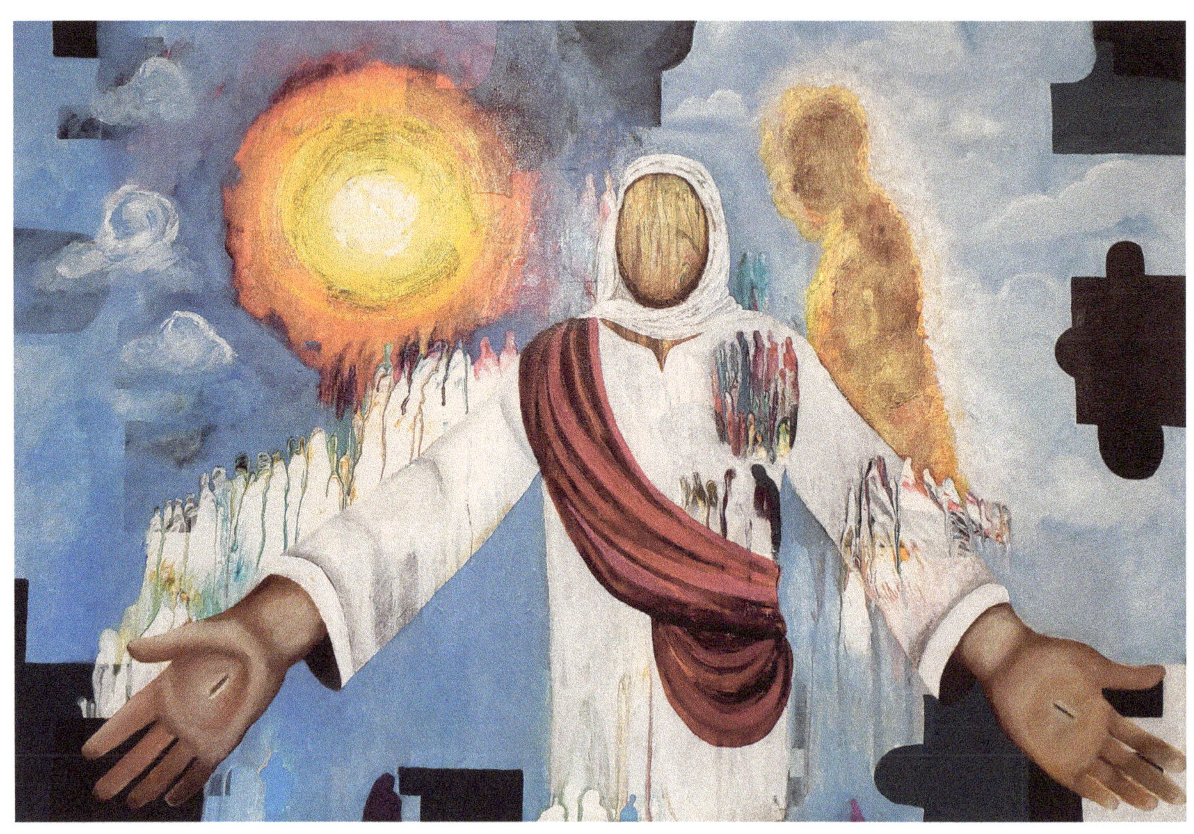

"Come"

Matthew 11:28-30 (AMP) "'Come to Me, all who are weary and heavily burdened [by religious rituals that provide no peace], and I will give you rest [refreshing your souls with salvation]. Take My yoke upon you and learn from Me [following Me as My disciple], for I am gentle and humble in heart, and you will find rest (renewal, blessed quiet) for your souls. For My yoke is easy [to bear] and My burden is light.'"

You don't have to carry all of the problems of the world on your shoulders. You weren't created to handle that kind of weight. Your body wasn't designed to handle ongoing stress and worry. Come and give those problems to God. He will carry the load, take the pressure off of you, and give you the rest you long for.

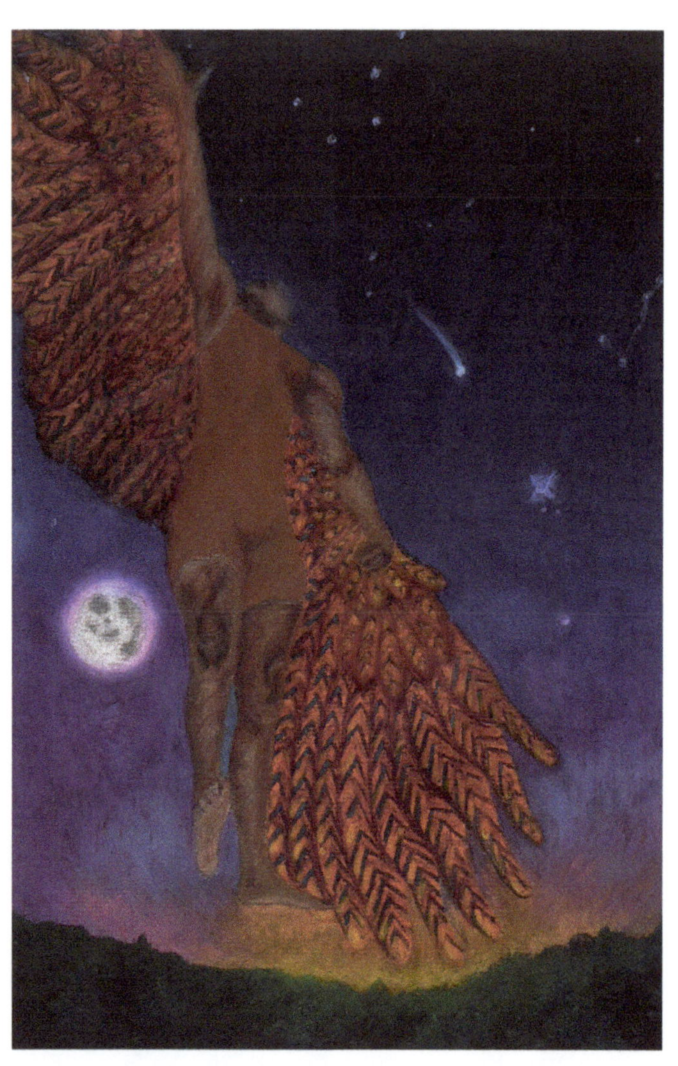

"New Strength—Night"

Isaiah 40:31 (AMP) "But those who wait for the LORD [who expect, look for, and hope in Him] Will gain new strength *and* renew their power; They will lift up their wings [and rise up close to God] like eagles [rising toward the sun]; They will run and not become weary, They will walk and not grow tired."

The phrase "wait for the Lord" appears eleven times in the books of Psalms and Isaiah. They all speak of the benefits received from waiting for the Lord. The verses state that God is our help and our shield. Those who wait on Him will inherit the land. He will hear your cry. But Isaiah 40:31 is the only verse that promises renewed strength to those who wait for the Lord. As a result of waiting for God, the renewed strength will give you endurance to proceed through the difficult and trying times of your life.

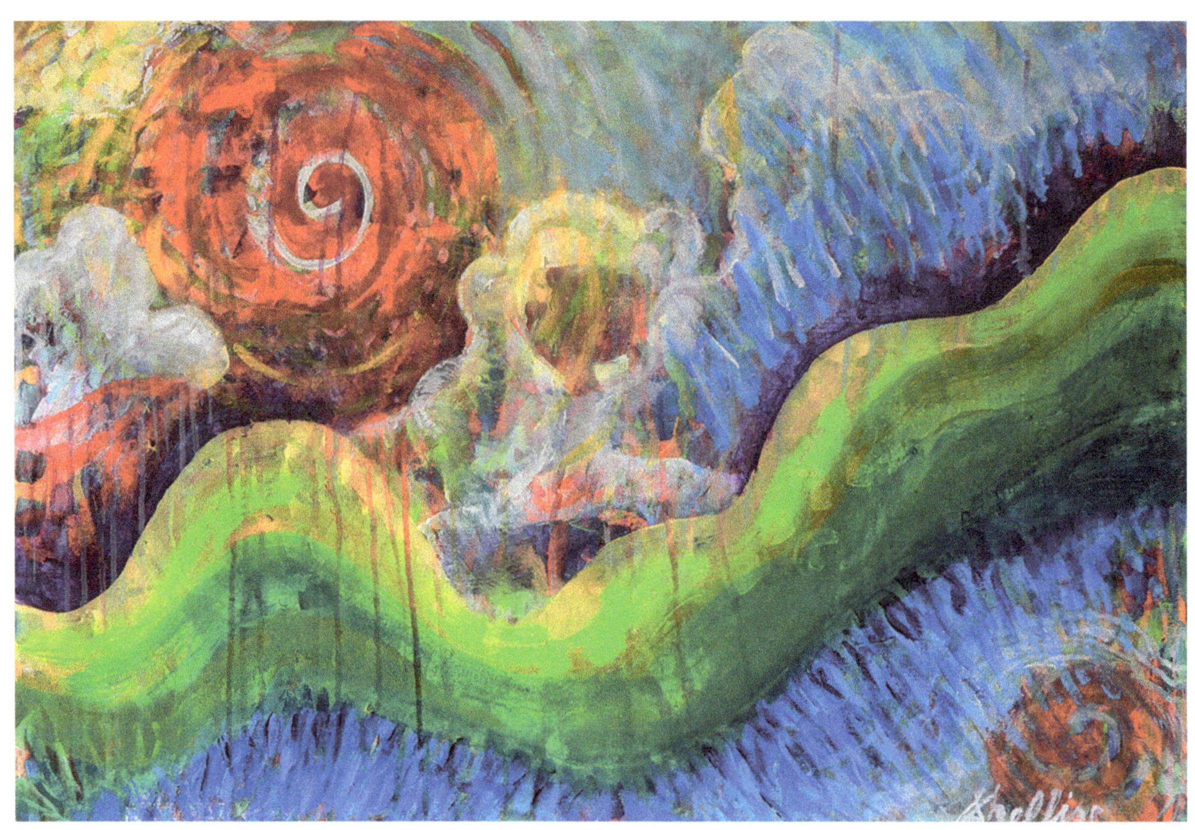

"Help"

Psalm 121:1-2 (AMP) "I will lift up my eyes to the hills [of Jerusalem]—From where shall my help come? My help comes from the LORD, Who made heaven and earth."

Life is full of valleys (low points) and hills (high points). It is comforting to know that when you are in the valley, you only have to lift your eyes toward heaven to receive the help you need. The valley you may be experiencing presently is a small thing to fix when it is the God who created the heavens and the earth who is fixing it. Give Him the problems that are challenging you. Rest knowing He will take care of everything. No problem is too great for our God.

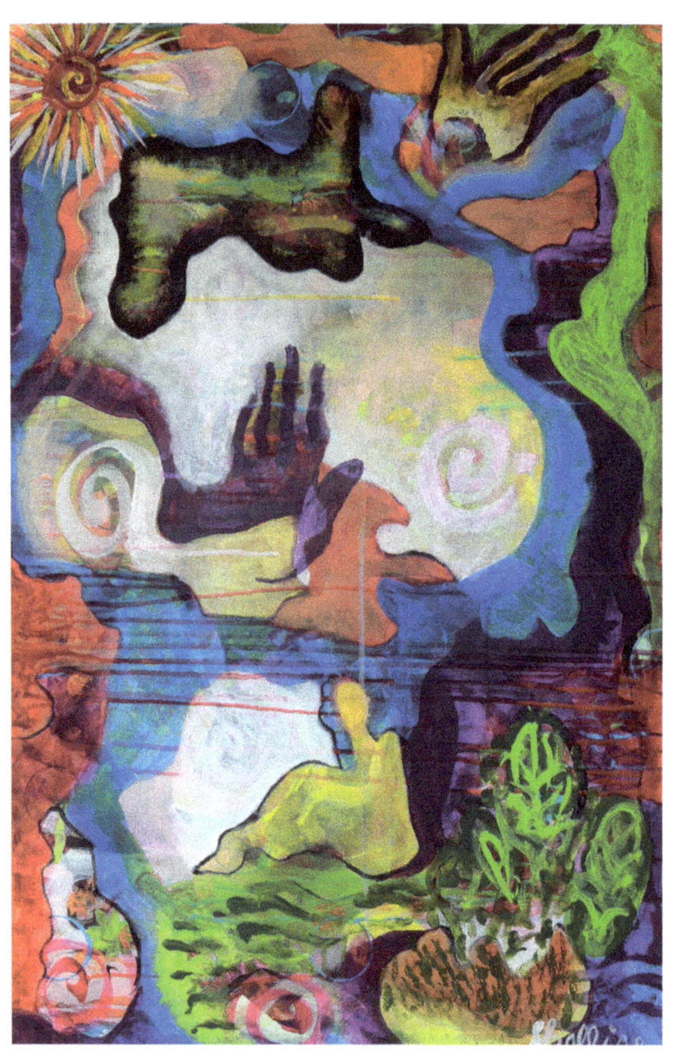

"Hand of God"

Joshua 4:24 (AMP) "'…so that all the peoples of the earth may know [without any doubt] *and* acknowledge that the hand of the LORD is mighty *and* extraordinarily powerful, so that you will fear the LORD your God [and obey and worship Him with profound awe and reverence] forever.'"

Deuteronomy 31:8 (AMP) "'It is the LORD who goes before you; He will be with you. He will not fail you or abandon you. Do not fear or be dismayed.'"

What does it mean to have the Lord's protection in life? It means that every day, you can walk safely and know that the Lord is always with you. You don't have to fear, because the Lord goes before you to prepare your way. He will never fail you or leave you. There are no situations too big for God to handle. He is all powerful. Hand your problems over to God today and rest in His mighty hands.

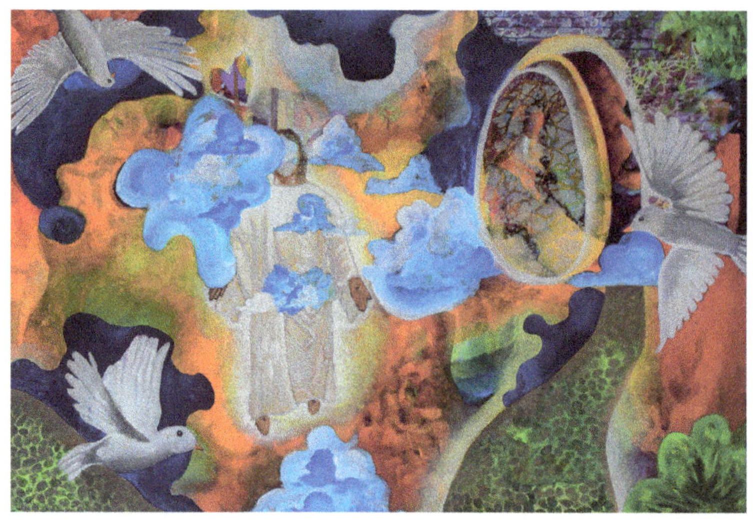

"Resurrection #2"

Matthew 28:5-7 (AMP) "But the angel said to the women, 'Do not be afraid; for I know that you are looking for Jesus who has been crucified. He is not here, for He has risen, just as He said [He would]. Come! See the place where He was lying. Then go quickly and tell His disciples that He has risen from the dead; and behold, He is going ahead of you into Galilee [as He promised]. There you will see Him; behold, I have told you.'"

1 Corinthians 15:6 (AMP) "After that He appeared to more than five hundred brothers and sisters at one time, the majority of whom are still alive, but some have fallen asleep [in death]."

Has fear occasionally taken hold of you? You're not expected to be perfect just because you're a believer. Even the women who followed Jesus felt fear when they arrived at the tomb and saw the angel. But like them, your fear will become joy as you remind yourself that God's Word is true. He will not fail to walk with you through your troubling situations.

Centuries before Christ was born, the Prophets declared that Jesus would be born of a virgin, perform extraordinary miracles, die, and rise from the dead. And rise He did! The angel announced it to the female believers. Not only did the disciples see Jesus after His resurrection, but so did five hundred others. So, you see, God always fulfills His promises. He will guide, protect, and never leave you. Rest assured that God will be with you through whatever you face.

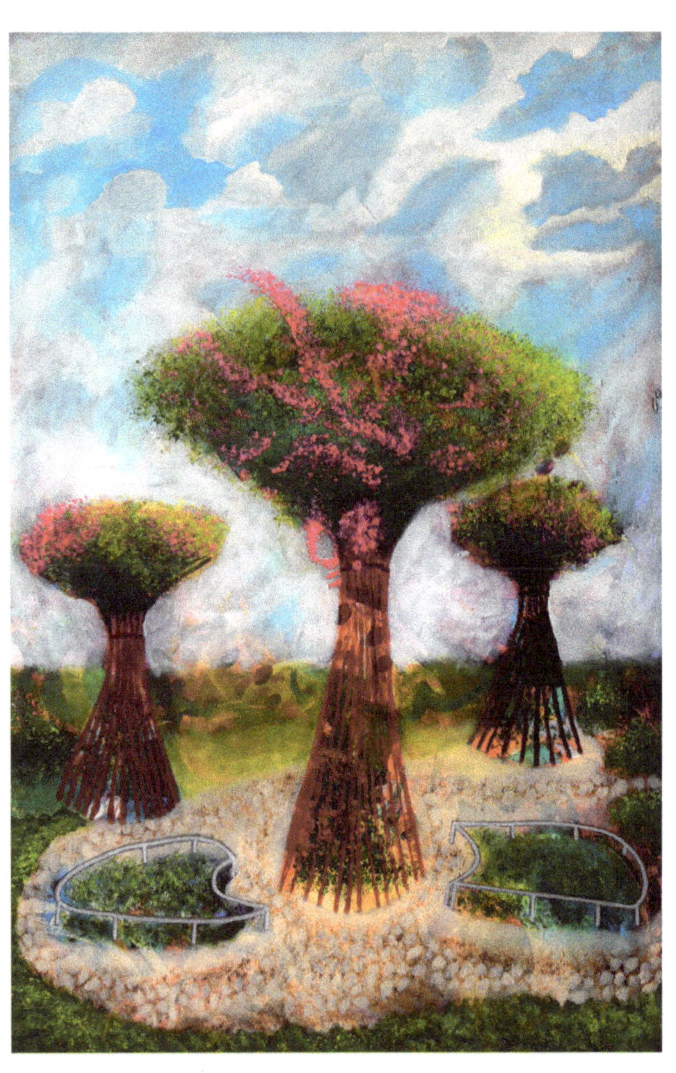

"Tranquility"

Philippians 4:6-7 (AMP) "Do not be anxious *or* worried about anything, but in everything [every circumstance and situation] by prayer and petition with thanksgiving, continue to make your [specific] requests known to God. And the peace of God [that peace which reassures the heart, that peace] which transcends all understanding, [that peace which] stands guard over your hearts and your minds in Christ Jesus [is yours]."

You don't have to be anxious about anything. Submit your specific requests regarding your situation to God. Thank Him in advance for the coming answer. Trust Him! He will provide the solution. In turn, He will give peace to your heart and mind.

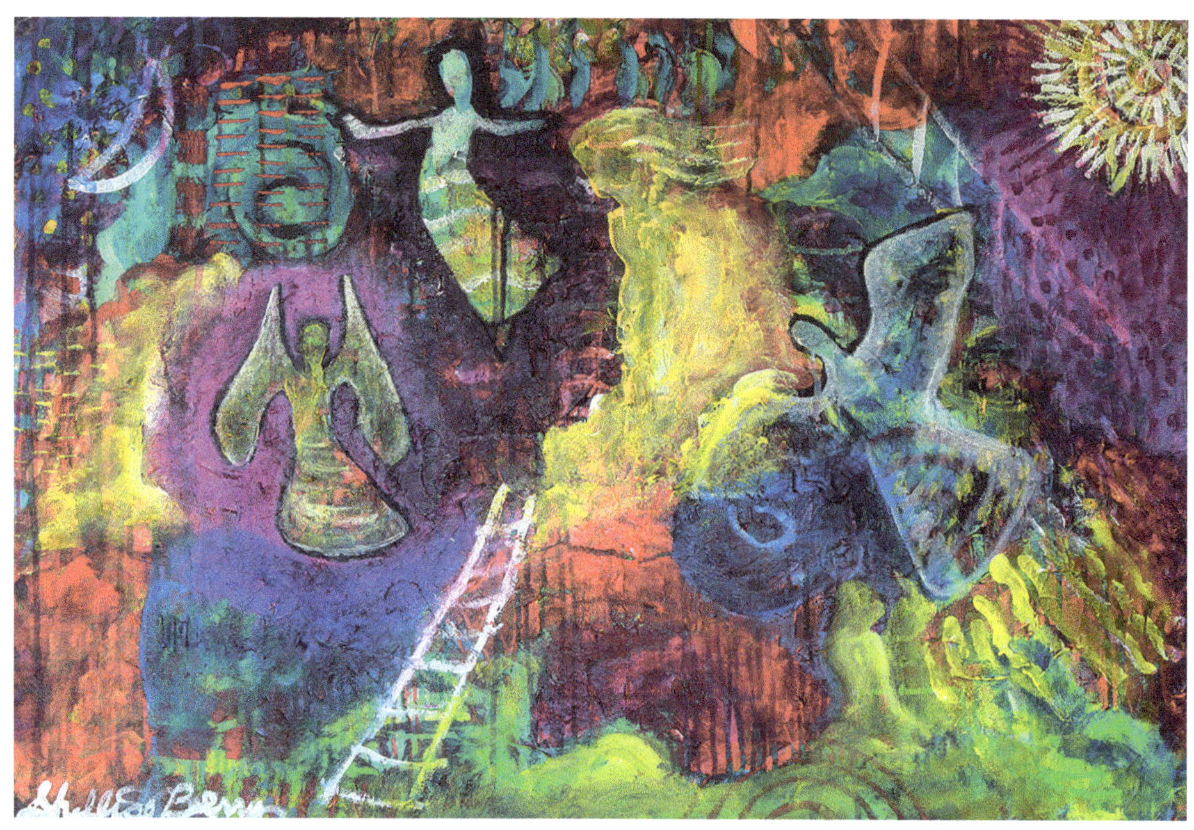

"Ascension"

Genesis 28:12 (AMP) "He dreamed that there was a ladder (stairway) placed on the earth, and the top of it reached [out of sight] toward heaven; and [he saw] the angels of God ascending and descending on it [going to and from heaven]."

In Jacob's dream, God provided a ladder for the angels to reach man. From the first time man disobeyed God, the relationship between God and man has been damaged. God devised a solution to restore man's relationship with Him. He sent His Son, Jesus, to pay the price for our sins (disobedience of God's will). Through the sacrifice of His life on the cross, Jesus became the ladder that allows us to reach God, thereby securing our place in heaven for eternity.

Bibliography

American Museum of Natural History. "New Study Doubles the Estimate of Bird Species in the World." Accessed October 27, 2020. https://www.amnh.org/about/press-center/new-study-doubles-the-estimate-of-bird-species-in-the-world/.

Laurie, Greg. "T.H.I.N.K.!!!" Accessed October 27, 2020. https://harvest.org/resources/gregs-blog/post/t-h-i-n-k/.

UCSB Scienceline. Accessed October 27, 2020. http://scienceline.ucsb.edu/getkey.php?key=3775#:~:text=The%20number%20of%20stars%20in,stars%20in%20the%20observable%20universe.

Worldometer. "World Population Clock." Accessed October 27, 2020. https://www.worldometers.info/world-population/.